John Milton

The Lycidas and Epitaphium Damonis of Milton

John Milton

The Lycidas and Epitaphium Damonis of Milton

ISBN/EAN: 9783743325890

Manufactured in Europe, USA, Canada, Australia, Japa

Cover: Foto ©ninafisch / pixelio.de

Manufactured and distributed by brebook publishing software (www.brebook.com)

John Milton

The Lycidas and Epitaphium Damonis of Milton

THE

LYCIDAS AND EPITAPHIUM DAMONIS

OF

MILTON

EDITED, WITH NOTES AND INTRODUCTION
(INCLUDING A REPRINT OF THE RARE LATIN VERSION OF
THE LYCIDAS BY WILLIAM HOGG, 1694), BY

C. S. JERRAM, M.A.

TRIN. COLL. OXON.

Λυκίδα φίλε, φαντὶ τὺ πάντες
συρίκταν ἔμεναι μέγ' ὑπείροχον ἔν τε νομεῦσιν
ἔν τ' ἀμητήρεσσι   THEOCR. *Idyll.* vii. 27

SECOND EDITION, REVISED

LONDON
LONGMANS, GREEN, AND CO.
1881

PREFACE

TO

THE SECOND EDITION.

THE Notes to this edition have been carefully revised, and several inaccuracies corrected. In making these improvements I have had the advantage of consulting Prof. Masson's three-volume edition of Milton's Poetical Works (1874) and Prof. Hales' *Longer English Poems*, which latter work, though published while my first edition was in progress, I had not then seen. One note (on *Lycidas* 163) has been entirely recast, a mature reconsideration of the passage having convinced me that the view I had previously taken is untenable. I have only to add, that the favourable opinions I have received, both publicly and privately, from many eminent English authorities induce me to hope that my book, in its emended form, may be welcomed by all students of Milton as a real contribution to this department of our literature.

C. S. J.

WINDLESHAM: *June* 1881.

PREFACE

TO

THE FIRST EDITION.

THE two following poems have been selected as the only specimens of Pastoral Elegy that Milton has given to the world. Besides the *Arcades* and the *Comus*—which are *dramatic*[1] pastorals—they are his sole contribution to a class of poetry which was in his age most fashionable, and whose influence is apparent in most of his poems, especially those of earlier date. The origin and history of the Pastoral, and its place in European literature, will form the subject of the first part of the following Introduction, in which I have endeavoured to give such preliminary information as may enable the reader

---

[1] An attempt was made to dramatise the *Lycidas* in a piece entitled *Lycidas, A Musical Entertainment*, which appears to have been performed at the Theatre Royal, Covent Garden, in 1767. It consists of Recitatives and Airs, with a couple of Choruses. For the Airs the words of the original are recast in short lines in a lyrical form; the following is a specimen, corresponding to *ll.* 113 foll. of the *Lycidas*:

How well could I have spared for thee
The Swains, who lean and flashy Songs
Grate on their Pipes of wretched Straw!
 The sheep look up and are not fed,
But swoln with the rank Mist they draw,
 Rot and the foul contagion spread—
Not so thy Flocks, O Shepherd dear;
Not so thy Songs, O Muse most rare!

For the credit of the play-going public of the last century it is to be hoped that this piece met with all the success it deserved.

to get some idea of the purpose and character of the *Lycidas* and the *Epitaphium Damonis* before entering upon a critical examination of them. With the former of these all Englishmen, who have even a moderate knowledge of the poetry of their own country, are probably more or less familiar; the latter is perhaps known only by name to many a student of Milton, whose acquaintance with him is confined to the English poems. All such will unite with me in grateful acknowledgments to Professor Masson for having rescued this touching elegy from its partial obscurity, by his notice of it as illustrating one of the most affecting passages in the early life of our great poet, and by his admirable translation into English hexameters, which by his kind permission I have been enabled to insert in this volume. And here, while I most gladly admit my many obligations to that eminent biographer of Milton, perhaps it is only fair to myself to say that the idea of including the *Epitaphium* was conceived by me long before the publication of his second volume. It was added not only because of the similarity of its subject and occasion to those of the *Lycidas*, but also from a belief that the study of Milton's Latin poetry, considered as a more or less successful imitation of ancient models, would prove eminently useful to those who are far enough advanced in scholarship to be able to translate the classical authors themselves with some degree of ease and fluency. Such a study, by way of occasional exercise, would be no bad training for young scholars in our public schools and elsewhere, if they came to the task furnished with some previous knowledge of the matter of the poems, such as the present edition supplies in the case of the *Epitaphium Damonis*. Here therefore the notes have been made as concise as possible; since I thought it unnecessary to dwell upon ordinary points of grammar, except where some unusual or doubtful construction might call for remark, and since I had explained many of the allusions in my previous commentary upon the *Lycidas*. As the greater number of the references are to Virgil and Theocritus, whose works every scholar is supposed to possess, I have not generally cited the passages *in extenso*; but in annotating the *Lycidas* some discretion has been exercised in this matter. Quotations from Latin, Greek, and sometimes from Italian authors, are mostly given in the original. In a few cases I have attempted a translation, where the point of the reference lay in the matter of the extract, and not in the grammatical form of expression.

In commenting upon both poems, I have tried to state clearly and without reserve the conflicting opinions of former editors upon disputed passages, fairly balancing the evidence and giving what I considered adequate reasons for choosing or rejecting any particular interpretation. In one or two instances I have been unwillingly compelled to leave the question doubtful, and in one at least (see note on *Lycidas*, 163) it was felt necessary to return to an older explanation, in spite of the fact that all recent editors have adopted the new one.[1] In every case I have aimed at so much conciseness as was compatible with a thorough examination of each

[1] See, however, Preface to the Second Edition.

point under discussion; for although I quite agree with Mr. Keightley[1] that brevity in a note is a thing most desirable, I know that it is highly unsatisfactory to the reader to find a difficulty unexamined or passed over, and to be put off with the *ipse dixit* of a commentator, when he expects, if not a solution of the matter in dispute, at least an impartial statement of diverse views. Besides supplying what is barely necessary for understanding the author's meaning, I have sought to give collateral information on points of English grammar and etymology, illustrated by references and quotations, and also to exhibit from certain lines in the *Lycidas* (especially *ll.* 113 foll.) Milton's relation to the history and religious opinions of his time. To avoid needlessly encumbering the notes, the bulk of such information has been placed in two Appendices at the end of the poem.

Among the various books consulted, I may mention the following:—

1. The editions of Milton's poems by Newton, Warton, and Todd, chiefly useful for references; also, Keightley's edition of 1859, and that by Mr. Browne, published in the Clarendon Series, 1870. The respective merits of all these are noticed in the Introduction (pp. 38-9).

2. Dictionaries of all kinds, English and foreign (including the latest edition of Johnson by Latham, and Wedgwood's *Dictionary of English Etymology*, 1872),

---

[1] Preface to his Edition of Milton's Poems.

PREFACE TO THE FIRST EDITION.

with other works, such as Earle's *Philology of the English Tongue*, Morris's *Outlines of English Accidence*, Marsh's *Lectures on the English Language*, &c. &c.

3. Masson's *Life of Milton* (to which I have already referred), Hallam's *History of Literature*, Warton's *History of English Poetry*, Scott's *Critical Essays* (1785), and several minor works bearing on the subjects under review.

As regards the text and various readings, I am greatly indebted to the courtesy of Mr. Aldis Wright, of Trinity College, Cambridge, who has been good enough to collate for me the MS. of *Lycidas* with Todd's list of readings and with the first printed editions, verifying all, and amending a few which that editor had incorrectly or insufficiently given.

I have also much pleasure in acknowledging my obligations to my friend, the Rev. James Moore, M.A., late Vicar of All Saints, Liverpool, for his careful revision of the MS. while it was in progress, for his help in arranging the materials of my Introduction, and for many valuable suggestions throughout the work.

Once or twice reference has been made to a certain Epitaph, which (as many readers may remember) was found by Professor Morley written in MS. at the end of a copy of the 1645 edition of Milton's poems, preserved in the King's Library of the British Museum. Not wishing to commit myself to an opinion either way upon the authorship of this poem, I have designated it simply as the *Miltonic Epitaph*. The whole story of its recovery and the arguments on Professor Morley's side of the controversy are given in his Introduction to *The King and the Commons*, published in 1869. At present the question is generally supposed to be settled against the Miltonic authorship, by the decision of those experts who assert that the handwriting is not Milton's, nor the signature J. M. There is at all events no dispute as to the date, which is 1647, and I have merely cited the poem as the work of a contemporary writer, and as undoubtedly 'Miltonic' in style and expression.

The Latin paraphrase of the *Lycidas*, by W. Hogg, is inserted at the suggestion of Mr. F. A. Paley of Cambridge, who has recently published a translation of the same poem. In his preface he alludes to Hogg's version of 1694, but regrets that he was unable to meet with a copy of it. There is a copy, possibly unique, of this paraphrase in the Library of the British Museum, preserved in a miscellaneous collection of pieces, chiefly of the 18th century. Most of the poems are in English, but one of them is a Latin version of the First Book of the *Paradise Lost*, by an unknown author, dated 1685. Hogg's translation is preceded by some Latin Elegiacs, *In Laudem Academiæ Cantabrigiensis*, not worth preserving, with a dedication to the Earl of Mulgrave. There is also an English address 'to the Reader,' explaining the circumstances of King's death, and of the production of the commemoratory verses (see *Introduction*, p. 2). Part of this address is worth quoting on account of its quaintness. 'Now he [Edward King] was a Person generally beloved in his Life, which made him so much lamented at his Death; which occasioned several Students

PREFACE TO THE FIRST EDITION. xiii

to pen lamentations on his Death,[1] *among whom was this Milton* and Clieveland. I was desired by others to make these two Translations, which was the occasion that I penned them. I was advised to put them in the Press, and that which encouraged me to adventure to do it was hopes that ingenious Gentlemen will communicate tokens of their kindness to me, for at this time my necessity is very great. These Poems will afford a high and innocent Recreation.' A version of Clieveland's elegy is, as the Latin title indicates, included in the volume; but I have not thought it worth while to reprint this in addition.

The English translation of the *Epitaphium Damonis*, by Dr. Symmons, is to be found in the Life of Milton appended to his edition of the Prose Works (1806). It is a fair specimen of the artificial literary style which prevailed during the 18th century; and it may be interesting to some readers to compare it with the version by Professor Masson, for the sake of contrast and variety.

[1] The italics are mine.

WOODCOTE HOUSE, WINDLESHAM:
May 1874.

CONTENTS.

	PAGE
PREFACE	v
INTRODUCTION	1
LYCIDAS	47
IDEM LATINE REDDITUM A GULIELMO HOGÆO	101
EPITAPHIUM DAMONIS	109
TRANSLATED BY DR. SYMMONS	126
THE SAME BY PROFESSOR MASSON	134

INTRODUCTION.

THE occasion which led to the production of the *Lycidas* is stated in the following heading prefixed to the poem by Milton himself: 'In this monody the Author bewails a learned Friend, unfortunately drowned in his passage from Chester on the Irish seas, 1637, and by occasion foretells the ruin of our corrupted Clergy, then in their height.'

This friend was Edward King, son of Sir John King, who was Secretary for Ireland under Elizabeth, James I., and Charles I. He was born at Boyle, Co. Roscommon; admitted as a lesser pensioner of Christ's College, Cambridge, at the age of fourteen, with his brother Roger aged sixteen, in 1626, Milton's third year, under the same tutor Chappell (*Lyc.* 36); and made Fellow by a royal mandate, dated June 10, 1630—an honour which Milton himself might well have expected. During his residence at Cambridge he wrote several copies of Greek and Latin verses (*Lyc.* 10) on special occasions, which are of no great merit, and was destined for holy orders (*Lyc.* 113 foll.). It would appear that by his moral worth and gentle bearing he had won the esteem of all his associates, though nothing is known of Milton's relations with him during their academic career, beyond what we gather from the poem before us. On August 10, 1637, as King was crossing from Chester to Dublin to visit his friends in Ireland (among whom was Chappell, now Dean of Cashel and Provost of Trinity College), the ship struck on a rock off the Welsh coast, and all on board are said to have perished (*Lyc.* 100). Accounts however vary about this, for Todd quotes from a preface by W. Hogg (1694), (whose Latin version of the *Lycidas* is included in this volume) a statement that 'some escaped in the boat,' and that they vainly tried to get King into it, so that he and the rest were drowned, 'except those only who escaped in the boat.' We do not know whence Hogg got this story: the authorised preface to the Cambridge verses of 1638 says, 'Dum alii vectores vitæ mortalis *frustra* satagerent,' which seems to imply that they all perished, though 'alii' (not being *ceteri*) does not necessarily mean this. The inscription goes on to say that King was in the act of prayer when the ship went down—a fact which could not have been known unless some one had survived to tell the tale. He was then aged twenty-five. Milton does not mention King's death in either of his letters to Diodati (Sept. 2 and 23, 1637); but later in Michaelmas Term he joined with other friends of the deceased in writing a series of memorial verses. He was then at Horton, where he also wrote the *Sonnet to a Nightingale* (1633), *L'Allegro* and *Il Penseroso*, *Arcades* and *Comus* (1634). The *Lycidas* is signed J. M., Nov. 1637 (but the Cambridge verses appeared early in the next year), and was republished with his full name and the title 'Poems on Several Occasions' in 1645, when the heading ' In this monody, &c.' was for the first time added. The whole collection had twenty-three Latin and Greek pieces and thirteen English, of which *Lycidas* came last: the first are entitled 'Edvardo King naufrago ab amicis mœrentibus, amoris et μνείας χάριν,' with the motto *Si recte calculum ponas, ubique naufragium est.* Among other names are Henry King, brother of Edward, and Beaumont of Peterhouse, afterwards better known. The verses are not worth preserving—a ' poetic *canaille*,' as Professor Masson calls them.

The name 'Lycidas' was a common one with the ancient bucolic poets, but perhaps the Seventh Idyll of Theocritus was especially in Milton's mind when he adopted it. The monody is cast in a form commonly known and designated as the 'pastoral;' it is not, however, strictly speaking, a pastoral, but a poem descriptive of college life under an allegory drawn from that of shepherds. It is well to make this distinction at the outset, in order to have some grounds for defending Milton against the charge of confusion and incongruity which certain critics (and notably Dr. Johnson, in his *Lives of the Poets*) have laid against him. The exact value of such criticism, as applied to the *Lycidas*, will be discussed in its proper place ; here it is enough to say that whatever may be the faults of the poem on this score (including the crowning one of all—the introduction of the Christian pastor side by side with the ideal shepherd), confusion of this kind did not begin with Milton, but had been the common practice of his predecessors in a style of composition which had long been degenerating from its primitive state of simplicity, and had now become an allowed medium for expressing opinions upon any sort of subject that might be present in the poet's mind. ✓ A brief review of pastoral poetry in its various stages from the time of Theocritus will best show how this change was brought about.

There is no reason for refusing the claims of the Syracusan bard to the honour of having originated this kind of poetry, if only we are careful to distinguish the pastoral of real life, such as the shepherds loved to practise in early times, from the artificial drafts of professed poets who made rural themes a vehicle for their imagination. Among these last we do not know for certain that Theocritus had any predecessors whose names can worthily be coupled with his own. Naeke (*Opuscula Philologica*, vol. i. p. 162) draws a good distinction between the old pastoral life and manners, which existed in the first ages of the world, and the artificial description of them which we call 'pastoral poetry.' He maintains that speculations, such as those prefixed to the Idylls on the origin of the pastoral,[1] really

---

[1] The Scholia on Theocritus (ed. Ziegler, 1867) say that, after some civil discord at Syracuse, the citizens held a festival to Artemis for having brought about a reconciliation, and that the rustics presented offerings and sang praises to the goddess in their own fashion; hence bucolic poetry had its beginning. Also that they afterwards continued the custom and sang for prizes of loaves and wallets full of seeds and skins of wine, with crowns on their heads, and horns on their foreheads, and

concern the olden times; but that the pastoral itself had no proper existence before Theocritus. He takes no notice of any difference between Theocritus and his successors in their method of treatment; and his remarks seem to imply that the *Idylls* of Theocritus were no more a picture of facts than Virgil's *Eclogues* or the Italian pastorals. It is indeed very hard to say how much in Theocritus is literal fact; but there is the plainest evidence that his scenes have been drawn from nature and from the shepherd-life of Sicily, and that they are the direct and first-hand presentation of actual shepherds singing of their flocks and of their loves, poetically but not allegorically. At the same time, his Idylls bear the trace of Alexandrian refinement, and of having been written, as Naeke says, 'non ad priscorum hominum ingenium sensumque,' &c., but for those 'qui tædio capti aliunde imaginem simplicitatis revocare student.' It was only natural that in those early times, when the conditions of human life were simple and uniform, and the shepherd's calling was followed by nearly all classes, the long hours of leisure should have been beguiled by song; and, as Lucretius [1] supposes, the whistling of the wind through the reeds might have suggested the first rude shepherd's pipe. Various degrees of skill would engender competition, and for this the rural festivities of Pan or Ceres would afford grand opportunities of display, which is probably the reason why the oldest theories on the subject ascribe the origin of pastoral poetry to such occasions. In course of time the best specimens would become known beyond the original rustic circle, and so professional poets began to adopt a similar mode of expression;

crooks in their hands. The above is stated as 'the true account'; some, however, maintain that pastoral poetry arose at Sparta during the Persian war, at a similar festival of Artemis and in a similar way; while others place its origin as far back as the time of Orestes, when he returned from Tauri with the image of Artemis and crossed from Rhegium to Tyndaris in Sicily, whereat the inhabitants sang praises to Artemis in their own rustic style, and thus gave rise to a regular custom.

[1] 'Et zephyri cava per calamorum sibila primum
Agrestes docuere cavas inflare cicutas.'—LUCR. 5, 1382 foll.

hence soon arose a distinct school of poetry, in which the poet and his friends are introduced in the dramatic form of shepherds, telling of their flocks and herds, their rustic amours, and the joys of a country life.[1]

But pastoral poetry was not destined to remain long in this state of uniform simplicity. The real and the dramatic characters soon became blended into one, and the shepherd was identified with the poet. Even in Theocritus we see the beginnings of this very natural confusion, for in the seventh Idyll the swain Simichidas professes his inferiority to Philetas and Asclepiades, actual poets of the day and the instructors of Theocritus, who, in fact, introduces himself under the name of Simichidas; but this Idyll is the only one which contains personal allusions to the poet, and in which real and imaginary names are intermingled. Passing on to the 'Επιτάφιος Βίωνος of Moschus, we find the same phenomenon more apparent; for there not only is the deceased bard lamented by name in the midst of a highly allegorical passage, and the real cause of his death by poison nakedly stated, but so transparent is the veil of pastoral allegory which disguises the personality of the poet, that Bion is represented as piping to his flocks and milking his goats at the same time that he is compared with Homer, Hesiod, and Pindar, with his own master Theocritus, and even with Moschus himself, in language which expressly intimates that something like a school of bucolic poetry was even thus early establishing itself in Sicily. Whether such an idea ever had any recognised existence, or had-reached any degree of maturity during the period of 200 years that intervened between Theocritus and Virgil, is a question we have no means of deciding; suffice it to say that in the time of the latter poet the terms 'Sicilian' and 'Syracusan' had come to be used as distinctive literary epithets of pastoral song (Virgil, *Ecl.* iv. 1;

* At secura quies et nescia fallere vita,
 Dives opum variarum, at latis otia fundis . . . .

Mugitusque boum mollesque sub arbore somni
Non absunt.'—VIRG. *G.* ii. 467.

vi. 1). This fact of itself shows how conventional the method of treating the subject had now become, and also prepares us for what we actually find when we examine the *Eclogues* of Virgil. The pastoral, which was at first a true and simple inspiration of nature, was already passing into an artificial stage in which it became the mouth-piece of general poetic utterance, and not seldom a mere toy for tiros in verse, 'as young birdes, that be newly crept out of the nest, by little first prove theyr tender wyngs, before they make a greater flyght.'[1] Such a fate indeed it was only too certain to incur when once it had taken its regular place in literature and lost its original simplicity. The poets who adopted the new fashion, though they assumed the character of shepherds, yet failed to attain the true pastoral result, since neither their own inclination nor surrounding influences favoured a consistent treatment. But in Virgil first of all the unreality and confusion of subject-matter and the general departure from primitive simplicity begin to be most conspicuous. His *Eclogues* are close imitations, often literal translations, of Theocritus; and in them we find the Greek pastoral applied to Roman life, and the scenery of Sicily transferred to the Mantuan district. Also the persistency with which shepherds bearing Greek names talk of Rome and the things of Rome, and adapt not only the pastoral imagery but even the very circumstances of the *Idylls* of Theocritus to the every-day occupations of Roman life, seems to prove that Virgil not merely recognised the Greek pastoral as the source of his inspiration, but sought to invest Theocritus himself with a Latin dress. And in numerous passages we cannot help seeing that he has allowed his excessive fondness of imitation to cramp his native originality, and to close his eyes to the open face of nature. At Rome Greek literature was a *beau idéal* of excellence, and Greek models were accepted as supreme; so that an aptness for applying the matter no less than the metre

---

[1] Spenser, *Epistle to Gabriell Harvey* (quoted also by Conington in his Introduction to Virgil's *Bucolics*).

of Greek poetry to Roman uses did not in those days appear to derogate in the least from the character of originality. Nevertheless Virgil, though he lived and breathed so fully in the atmosphere of Greece, and reproduced with such exactness the tastes and impressions he had there imbibed, copied as one who brought with him native insight and vision, and had the power of impressing his own stamp upon much that he had gathered from others. The confusion of the pastoral may be considered as fully developed in the *Eclogues*, though oftentimes so perfect is the poet's art, and so exquisite his grace, that we may be led to forget or even to reconcile ourselves to what he has done in this direction. Henceforth pastoral poetry is no more than a particular mode of poetical expression, and has nothing in common with Theocritus beyond its outside form.[1] It seems strange indeed that a people like the Romans, claiming descent from a pastoral ancestry and nursed by a regular recurrence of festivals in pastoral recollections, should afterwards have been almost wholly indifferent to the cultivation of this class of poetry; yet the later Roman bucolic poets, such as Calpurnius and Nemesianus, occupy but a low place among the post-Augustan authors, and need only be mentioned as specimens to show how little regard was paid to the Pastoral for some time after the days of Virgil. Their poetry, which invests political subjects with a pastoral dress, is miserably unreal, and, though obviously Virgilian in its style and aim, is wholly destitute of the master's power and elegance. It may be interesting to notice here in passing an eclogue (*Conflictus Veris et Hiemis, sive Cuculus*) by the Venerable Bede, which was one of the few and scattered pastoral reminiscences during the long and dreary period which intervened between the old and the new epochs of literature.

From what has been said it appears that there may be two kinds of pastoral—one real and the other allegorical: the first

---

[1] For a fuller and nearly exhaustive criticism of Virgil's *Eclogues*, in their relation to the *Idylls* of Theocritus, see Conington's Introduction to the *Bucolics*, in vol. i. of his edition of Virgil.

gives an actual representation of rural life in any country whatever, such as we partially find in the *Idylls* of Theocritus, while among our own poets perhaps Ben Jonson, in his *Sad Shepherd*, has approached most nearly to this primitive type. The second class is represented by Spenser and his contemporaries, its object being to disentangle the poet from all local and surrounding associations, and to place him in such a state of ideal freedom as shall afford full scope for his imagination. For this the fiction of some Arcadia, a kind of visionary land, was most suitable, where the poet, in shepherd guise, could adapt to his purpose as much of pastoral life as he saw fit. And although Spenser, in the opening lines of the *Faery Queen*, gives notice of changing his 'oaten reeds for trumpets stern,' and for 'knights and ladies gentle deeds,' much of the pastoral nevertheless shows itself even here. Whatever the theme might be, it was thrown by the poetical fashion of the time into an imaginary world, and an ideal scene was fitted to it.

The earliest modern pastorals are Portuguese,[1] in or even before the fourteenth century. They mainly deal with the passion of love in its relation to the ideal felicity of shepherd life. Spain followed in the same course; but the adoption of the fashion by the Italians, whose language was more widely known, started an epoch of great popularity for this kind of composition in Europe. Sannazaro wrote his *Arcadia* in 1502, and the *Piscatory Eclogues*,[2] which are in Latin and very Virgilian, appeared about 1520. Soon afterwards began the regular pastoral drama, of which *Il Sagrifizio* of Beccari, in 1554, was the first specimen. This, as Hallam thinks, may have been suggested by the 'Sicilian Gossips' (*Adoniazusæ*) of Theocritus, where there is the germ of a dramatic action in the dialogue. George de Montemayor, who, by his *Diana*, made

---

[1] Except the French *pastourelles*, which were love dialogues in alternate stanzas and in pastoral character.

[2] Dr. Johnson (*Rambler*, 1750) observes that, as the range of pastoral is narrow, Sannazaro tried to vary his imagery by depicting the sea and fishermen; but the sea having less variety than the land, and being less known to the generality of men, is therefore less fit for pastoral.

this kind of poetry fashionable in Spain, followed Sannazaro, but improved upon him by giving more variety, more passion, more reasoning, and a more connected story. Then followed Lope de Vega with his *Arcadia*, about the end of the sixteenth century. Towards 1580 came Tasso's *Aminta*, and in 1585 Guarini's *Pastor Fido*, containing musical choruses, 'the prototypes of the Italian Opera which added recitatives to the choruses.'

In 1690 the Society of Arcadians was founded at Florence by Crescentini. They assumed all the accessories of Greek pastoral, and took as their device the pipe of seven reeds bound with laurel; and their president was designated 'custode generale.'[1] Their influence was great in purifying the national taste; and though the poetry rather lacked power of feeling, its natural imagery and pastoral character have invested it with a charm and beauty which to the imaginative reader is quite irresistible. From Italy the fashion passed to England about the sixteenth century, when travel led the way to knowledge, and translations began to be made. Though the influence of Italian poetry upon English literature goes back at least to Chaucer, who translated many lines from the Italian, and probably borrowed his *Palamon and Arcite* and his *Troilus* from the *Theseida* and *Filóstrato* of Boccaccio respectively, yet it was not till much later that Italian poets and romances were popularly known in avowed translations. Ascham, in his *Scholemaster* (1589), complains of them as 'carrying the will to vanitie and marring good manners.' Boccace's novels were translated by W. Paynter in 1566, and Burton, in his *Anatomy of Melancholy*, mentions the reading aloud of them as a winter evening's diversion. A translation of Ariosto's *Orlando Furioso* by Harvington appeared in 1590, and one of Tasso's *Gerusalemme Liberata*, probably by Carew, in 1593.

The first English pastorals were Barkley's Eclogues (1514), chiefly moral and satirical, with little rural scenery. They were

[1] From Hallam's *History of European Literature*, vol. ii.

modelled on Petrarch's XII. Eclogues (1350), which were the first modern Latin bucolics, and on Mantuan (1402). And these modern Latin pastorals became so much admired that a collection of thirty-eight of them was printed at Basel in 1546. Mantuan was read and taught as a classic : see Shaksp., *Love's Labour Lost*, iv. 2, where Holofernes quotes a line of his and says, 'Old Mantuan ! old Mantuan ! who understandeth thee not loves thee not.' In 1563 came Googe's *Eglogs*,[1] *Epitaphs, and Sonnets*, and this abundance of pastorals is probably traceable to the fascination of the Italian poets. Spenser's Eclogue *December* is a literal rendering from the French of Clément Marot. (Warton's *Hist. of English Poetry*, and *Critique on the Faery Queen*.)

In the Elizabethan age pastoral poetry was a popular delight. Bishop Hall, *Prologue to Satires*, 1597, exclaims—

> Would ye but breathe within a wax-bound quill,
> Pan's sevenfold pipe, some plaintive pastoral;

and in his first satire he complains that he cannot

> Under everie bank and everie tree
> Speak rimes unto mine oaten minstrelsie.

In his *History of English Poetry* Warton remarks : ' This familiarity with the pagan story was owing to the numerous English versions of them. Translations occupied every pen, and acquired a general notoriety. Learned allusions were no longer obscure [2] to common readers; but their extravagances

---

[1] Petrarch introduced the form *Æglogue* for *Eclogue*, imagining the word to be derived from αἴξ (αἰγός), 'a goat,' and to mean 'the conversation of goatherds.' But, as Dr. Johnson observes in his *Life of A. Philips*, it could only mean 'the talk of goats.' Such a compound, however, could not even exist, as it would be αἰγο-λογία, if anything. *Eclogæ* (ἐκ-λογαί) of course mean simply Selected Pieces, a name afterwards given to the poems which Virgil himself called by the descriptive name *Bucolica*.

[2] The chief translations of the classics after 1550 are Virgil's *Æneid*, by Phaier (1558); by Stanihurst (1583); the *Culex*, by Spenser (1591); Ovid's *Metamorphoses*, by Golding (1565); *Epistles*, by Turberville (1567); *Tristia*, by Churchyard (1580); Horace's *Epistles* and *Satires*, by Drant (1567); Homer,

were imitated, and not their natural beauties.' Again: 'When the queen paraded through a country town, almost every pageant was a pantheon. When she paid a visit at the house of any of her nobility, on entering the hall she was saluted by the Penates, and conducted to her privy chamber by Mercury. . . . At dinner select transformations of Ovid's *Metamorphoses* were exhibited in confectionery. . . . When she condescended to walk in the garden, the lake was covered with Tritons and Nereids; the pages of the family were converted into wood nymphs, who peeped from every bower, and the footmen gambolled over the lawns in the figure of satyrs.[1] . . . When her majesty hunted in the park, she was met by Diana, who, pronouncing our royal prude to be the brightest paragon of unspotted chastity, invited her to groves free from the intrusions of Actæon. . . . In one of the fulsome interludes at court, the singing boys of her chapel presented the story of the three rival goddesses on Mount Ida, to which her majesty was ingeniously added as a fourth; and Paris was arraigned in form for adjudging the golden apple to Venus, which was due to the queen alone.' (Warton's *Hist. of Eng. Poetry*, ed. 1824, vol. iv. p. 323.)

Besides the classics and the Italian tales, Gothic romance still held its ground. 'Giants, dragons, and enchanted castles, borrowed from the magic storehouse of Boiardo, Ariosto, and Tasso, began to be employed by the epic muse. The Gothic and pagan fictions were blended and incorporated' (*ib.*); and we find in Sidney's *Arcadia* an application of the Italian pastoral to feudal manners, and so fashionable did pastoral writings soon become that the language of courtiers with all its false and tawdry finery was put into the mouths of simple shepherds. Spenser, whose *Shepheard's Calendar* (1579) is the masterpiece of all pastorals in that age, brought his treatment nearer to the truth of nature; yet the Doric rusticity of the dia-

by Chapman (1604-14). Queen Elizabeth herself translated Seneca's *Hercules Œtæus*.

[1] See account of the pageant at Kenilworth in Scott's novel of that name.

logue is somewhat repulsive to modern ears ; and this, which was native to Theocritus, is borrowed, not always [1] correctly, by his English imitator.

In 1590 appeared Sidney's *Arcadia*, one of the most beautiful efforts of English fancy in that age—not exactly a pastoral, since it has far less to do with shepherds than with courtiers and knights, though the idea might have been suggested by the popularity of the *Diana* of Montemayor, to which allusion has been already made. In the preface of his edition of the *Arcadia* (1867) Mr. Friswell says : ' The scene is laid in a fabulous and semi-pagan Greece, where young people wander in woods, kill lions and bears, fall in love, believe in Christianity and heathen gods, wear armour like the Tudor knights, and fight with Helots and Lacedæmonians, in a most confusing way.' It would now, perhaps, be thought very tedious, but it is less pedantic than most books of that time, and its popularity was great in the days of Shakspere and for years afterwards (Hallam, vol. ii. p. 216). Early in the seventeenth century appeared the *Faithful Shepherdess* of Fletcher (the forerunner of *Comus*), Browne's *Britannia's Pastorals* (1613), also well known to Milton, and the *Sad Shepherd* of Jonson.

Touching the influence of Spenser on succeeding poetry, Professor Masson (vol. i. p. 410 foll.) remarks that about 1630 there was 'a distinct Spenserian School,' partly of professed and partly of unconscious disciples. As the poetry of Spenser is ' as nearly poetry in its essence as any that ever was,' a resemblance to him was thought a warrant of poetic quality. This is seen in Chapman, Jonson, Drayton, and others, Shakspere being an exception, *sui generis*, and of no school. But there were also those who purposely studied Spenser, made him their avowed model, and cultivated his forms of poetry—the pastoral and the descriptive allegory ; and among these W. Browne and Giles and Phineas Fletcher stand most prominent.

---

[1] For the mistakes which Spenser has made as to the meaning of some of the old words he uses, see notes by Skeat on the two concluding eclogues of the *Shepheard's Calendar*.

Browne's *Brit. Pastorals* (1613-1616) are cast very closely in pastoral form, and are a story of shepherds amid scenes of English country life, full of luxuriant natural descriptions, with only an occasional flight to higher subjects. Spenser is acknowledged several times by name, but traces of other poets (especially of Du Bartas [1]) may be discerned. The *Shepherd's Pipe*, of seven eclogues (1614), is a simpler poem, and one of equal skill. Of Giles Fletcher there only remains *Christ's Victory over Death* (1610), which is very Spenserian. Phineas Fletcher's two great poems are the *Piscatory Eclogues*, where fishermen take the place of shepherds, and the *Purple Island*, a poem describing the anatomy of the human body under an image indicated by that name. Both were published at Cambridge soon after 1632.

The old criticisms on what the pastoral ought to be may be divided into two classes, each of which failed, though in a different way, of hitting the mark. Those who insisted upon a 'golden age,' simple manners, mean sentiments, and the like, confused the pastoral of real life, which had long ceased to exist (if it ever did exist after Theocritus), with the changed artificial growth which had sprung out of it. Those on the other hand who avoided this particular mistake, but forbade all allusions to politics or religion as foreign to the nature of the pastoral, forgot that all pastoral poets after Virgil's time had admitted such allusions, and by so doing had, as it were, legalised them; and these same critics fell into the totally distinct error of allowing too wide a definition of this sort of poetry, as if any rural poem whatever were *ipso facto* a pastoral. Having briefly drawn this distinction, let us now examine by way of

---

[1] Sylvester translated the *Divine Weeks and Works* of Du Bartas in 1605, which was very popular till 1650, but afterwards ceased to be read. When Milton was a boy, everybody was reading it. The first part of the poem is called 'The First Week,' or 'Birth of the World,' and it is divided into seven days or cantos. The Second Week contains the Bible history as far as the Kings and Chronicles, also divided into days, each corresponding to an epoch and headed with a name (Adam, Noah, &c.). Four days are complete; the rest are unfinished.

illustration a few of the opinions of successive critics, remarking upon them as we proceed.

In the Preface to John Fletcher's *Faithful Shepherdess* we read : ' A pastoral is a representative of shepherds and shepherdesses with their actions and passions, which must be such as may agree with their natures ; at least, not exceeding former pictures and vulgar traditions. They are not to be adorned with any art but such as nature is said to bestow, such as singing and poetry, or such as experience may teach them, as the virtues of herbs, &c.' Again, Drayton, in his Preface to the *Pastorals*, observes : ' The subject of pastoral, as the language of it, ought to be poor, silly, and of the coarsest woof in appearance, yet the highest and noblest matters of the world may be shadowed forth in them. The chief law of pastoral is *decorum*, and that not to be exceeded without leave, or, at least, fair warning.' Pope, in the Introduction to his *Pastorals* (1704), gives a *résumé* of the opinions of preceding critics, the chief of which are that ' Pastoral is an image of the golden age,' so that ideal and not actual shepherds have to be described. The principal points to be observed are ' simplicity, brevity, and delicacy.' ' The fable simple, the manners not too polite nor too rustic, the thoughts plain—the expression humble, yet as pure as the language will afford, neat but not florid, easy yet lively.' The joyous side of shepherd life and not the miseries should be shown. The Eclogues should be various, each having its own particular beauties. In the *Guardian* (1713) pastoral poetry is spoken of as describing a state of early innocence and joy, ' where plenty begot pleasure, and pleasure begot singing, and singing begot poetry, and poetry begot pleasure again.' Simplicity must be pourtrayed, but troubles should be concealed, except such small annoyances as merely set off the general happiness of the state. The shepherds need not, however, be ' dull and stupid ;' they may have ' good sense and even wit, provided it be not too gallant and refined ;' but they must not ' make deep reflections,' which are to be left to the reader. The reasons why we are pleased with pastoral are threefold—

'love of ease,' 'approbation of innocence and simplicity,' and 'love of the country;' and all these are natural to man. Theocritus is the great master of pastoral; Virgil sacrifices simplicity to nobleness and sublimity, and some of his *Eclogues* are not properly pastorals at all. The Italians are 'fond of surprising conceits and far-fetched imaginations,' as is shown in Tasso's *Aminta* and Guarini's *Pastor Fido*. 'The French are so far from thinking abstrusely that they often seem not to think at all;' 'they fall into the manner of their country, which is gallantry,' and the dresses and manners of their shepherds are like those of a court and ball-room. The English have too servilely copied the Greek and Roman pastorals; Spenser and A. Philips have succeeded best, since they have 'not only copied but improved the beauties of the ancients.' The manner of the ancients should be followed, but deviations as to climate, customs, and the soil and its products, are to be recommended. The theology of the Pagan pastoral may be retained, where 'universally known; and all else should be made up of our own rustical superstition of fairies, goblins, &c.—since no man can be delighted with the imitation of what he is ignorant of.' On April 27, 1713 (*Guardian*, No. 40), appeared a mock comparison of Philips's with Pope's *Pastorals*, really written by Pope himself, in which he gave the palm of superiority to his own poems under pretence of preferring those of his rival. The whole production is ironical, and it ends by asserting of Pope's *Pastorals* that 'they are by no means pastorals, but something better.' Here we must not omit to notice Gay's burlesque pastorals, entitled the *Shepherd's Week*, both because many of his remarks, though ironically uttered, really bear on the matter before us, and because there has been from time to time so much ludicrous misconception as to their object and character. We make the following extracts from the Proeme to the *Shepherd's Week*, which appeared in 1714: 'Great marvel hath it been that in this our island of Britain no poet hath hit on the right simple eclogue after the true ancient guise of Theocritus before this mine attempt. . . . My love to my country much pricketh me forward to describe aright the manners of our own honest ploughmen; albeit not ignorant am I what a rout and rabblement of critical gallimawfry hath been made by certain young men concerning I wist not what Golden Age and other outrageous conceits to which they would confine pastoral. This idle trumpery unto that ancient Doric shepherd Theocritus was never known. It is therefore my purpose to set forth before thee a picture of thy own country. . . . Thou wilt not find my shepherdesses idly piping on oaten reeds, but milking the kine, tying up the sheaves, &c. Spenser I must acknowledge a bard of sweetest memorial; yet hath his shepherd's boy at times raised his rustic reed to rhymes more rumbling than rural. Diverse grave points hath he also handled of churchly matter, to great clerks only appertaining. His names [are] indeed right simple and meet for the country (Lobbin, Cuddy, &c.), some of which I have made bold to borrow. . . . The language of my shepherds is such as is neither spoken by the country maiden nor the courtly dame, having too much of the country to be fit for the court, too much of the court to be fit for the country. . . . But here again much comfort ariseth in me from the hopes that some lover of simplicity shall arise who shall render these mine eclogues into such more modern dialect as shall be then understood.'[1]

In the pieces which follow, Gay's object was to ridicule pastoral itself by presenting a homely and often coarse picture of rustic life as a set-off against the 'golden age' view we have mentioned; and in doing so he claims simply to be going back to Theocritus, the fountain-head of all bucolic poetry, who was himself faithful to nature. Nor can it be denied that Gay

---

[1] Dr. Johnson (*Life of Gay*) says that Pope 'is supposed to have incited Gay to write the *Shepherd's Week*, to show that, if it be necessary to copy nature with minuteness, rural life must be exhibited such as grossness and ignorance have made it. The Pastorals are introduced by a Proeme, written in imitation of obsolete language. But the effect of reality and truth became conspicuous, even when the intention was to show them grovelling and degraded. These Pastorals became popular, and were read with delight by those who had no interest in the rivalry of the poets, nor knowledge of the critical dispute.'

does in this respect present us with a superficial copy of his alleged model in almost everything but the ridiculous names (Blowselinda, Bowsybæus, &c.) he gives to some of his characters, which are not at all after the style of those adopted by Theocritus. How then is it that Gay's pastorals are on the whole an evident burlesque, while those of Theocritus are as evidently real?· It cannot be merely a question of coarseness as contrasted with refinement, for there are indecencies in some of the Idylls to which no parallel can be found in the *Shepherd's Week*. As a poet of course Theocritus has the advantage; but this does not make all the difference between them. The solution seems to be in some way as follows. Both poets described actual facts of rural life and in homely language; but the kind of rural life Theocritus had to describe was very different from that which came under the notice of Gay. 'Thou wilt not find my shepherdesses idly piping on oaten reeds, but milking the kine, tying sheaves,' &c. Just so; but the shepherds of Theocritus *did* pipe as well as milk and bind sheaves; and if they had not piped, or if no shepherds had ever done so, the production which we call Pastoral Poetry would never have existed. This does not consist merely in a description of rustic manners.[1] To us it is purely artificial, and has been so in all countries ever since Virgil's time; but to Theocritus and his contemporaries it was a reality —a substantially correct reproduction of the doings, feelings, occupations, and utterances of the Sicilian shepherds — and afterwards but too often an ungainly mimicry of what once had

[1] From not observing this fact, Crabbe made the *genuine* mistake embodied in the following lines from his poem *The Village* (1783):—
'On Mincio's banks in Cæsar's bounteous reign,
If Tityrus found the golden age again,
Must sleepy bards the flattering dreams prolong,
Mechanic echoes of the Mantuan song?

From Truth and Nature shall we widely stray
Where Virgil, not where Fancy, leads the way?
Yes, thus the Muses sing of happy swains,
Because the Muses never knew their pains . . . . .
By such examples taught I paint the cot
As Truth will paint it, and as bards will not.'

life and reality. The shepherd's pipe, which was at first real, became afterwards a sham; and the poetry met with much the same fate. Owing to the nature of its climate and its manners, England is not a country in which shepherds could practise piping and singing like the Dorian swains; and perhaps neither the genius nor the language of the English race would ever have fostered anything like the true ancient pastoral amongst us.[1]

Of those critics, who fell into the error of identifying the pastoral with rural poetry in general, Dr. Johnson may be fairly taken as the representative. In the *Rambler* he remarks, 'The true definition of a pastoral is a poem in which any action or passion is represented by its effects upon a country life, and has nothing peculiar but its confinement to rural imagery, without which it ceases to be pastoral.' Hence he thinks those writers are wrong who insist upon a golden age, meanness of sentiment and language, and confinement to persons of low rank.[2] Still the interest should be centred in rural life, and therefore should not contain allusions to the Church or State, or 'lamentations on the death of some illustrious person, whom when once the poet has called a shepherd he has no longer any labour upon his hands, but can make the lilies wither and the sheep hang their heads, without any art or learning, genius or study.' On the misconception involved in refusing to admit political allusions into the pastoral we have already remarked (p. 13); that there is the essence of truth in the last quoted sentence (*minus* the sarcasm) every reader will allow. We will close this part of our subject by citing a still more sarcastic

---

[1] 'In England every poet who has tried to play on the Doric pipe has sounded a false note. There is nothing in our damp island atmosphere, or in our own character, to favour that easy, contented, grasshopper life which still marks the peoples of the South.'—*Quarterly Review*, July 1873.

[2] He instances 'the Dorick' of Spenser's *Shepheard's Calendar*, 'a mangled dialect which no human being could ever have spoken,' and quotes the opening of the 9th Eclogue,—

'Diggon Davie! I bidde her god daye;
Or Diggon her is, or I missaye,' &c.

—which Pope affected to admire in his ironical essay in the *Guardian*, No. 40.

utterance of the same critic, in his life of A. Philips (1781), which nevertheless gives us a perfectly true account of the reasons why the writing of pastorals became so fashionable. 'At the revival of learning in Italy, it was soon discovered that a dialogue of imaginary swains might be composed with little difficulty; because the conversation of shepherds excludes profound or refined sentiment, and for images and descriptions satyrs, fauns, &c., were always within call; and woods, rivers, &c., supplied variety of matter, which having a natural power to soothe the mind did not quickly cloy it.' Add to this the well-known charms of the country and its associations, and the relief which these afford from the turmoils of life, to the imagination at least, if not always in reality, and we shall cease to wonder at the vitality of a species of composition which held its ground for so many centuries, though it has now, perhaps for ever, passed away.

Hence it will appear that even if *Lycidas* were a formally cast Pastoral, ample license by precedents would be allowed for the method in which Milton has treated his subject. We are now in a position to consider a few of the criticisms which have been passed upon the poem itself. That of Dr. Johnson in his *Lives of the Poets* is the best known and the most unfavourable of all. In his *Life of Milton* he writes :—'The diction is harsh, the rhymes uncertain, and the numbers unpleasing . . . . . not the effusion of real passion, which runs not after remote allusions and obscure opinions. . . . . . Where there is leisure for fiction there is little grief. . . . . . No nature, for there is no truth; no art, for there is nothing new. Its form is pastoral, easy, vulgar, and therefore disgusting. . . . . . When Cowley tells Hervey that they studied together, it is easy to suppose how much he must miss the companion of his labours; but what image of tenderness can be excited by these lines: "We drove afield, &c."? . . . . . Though the representation may be allegorical, the true meaning is so uncertain and remote that it is never sought, because it cannot be known when it is found. Among the flocks, &c., appear the heathen deities, Jove, &c. He who thus grieves will excite no sympathy; he who thus praises will confer no honour.' Again—'With these trifling fictions are mingled the most awful and sacred truths. . . . . . The shepherd is now a feeder of sheep, and afterwards a superintendent of a Christian flock—an approach to impiety of which, however, I believe the writer not to have been conscious. . . . . . No man could have fancied that he read *Lycidas* with pleasure had he not known the author.' It should in the first place be understood that in Milton's day English poetry had not been brought under the kind of criticism to which it has since been subjected, and that therefore we must view the *Lycidas* in relation to its age. But whatever incongruities a harsh and prosaic test may elicit, other critics even of Dr. Johnson's own time have held very different opinions respecting the melody, tenderness, and grandeur of this charming poem.[1] Thyer (1785) observes that 'what gives the greatest grace to the whole poem is the natural and agreeable wildness and irregularity which runs through it, than which nothing could be better suited to express the affection which Milton had for his friend. Grief is eloquent, but not formal.' Hurd, though he sees 'no extraordinary *wildness and irregularity* in the conduct of this little poem,' remarks, 'There is a very original air in it, owing not to disorder in the plan, but to the variety of the metre. Milton's ear was a good second to his imagination.' On Johnson's comparison of *Lycidas* with Cowley's *Elegy*, Scott (*Critical Essays*, 1785) says, 'Cowley speaks of Hervey *in propria persona*; Milton is *pro tem.* a rustic poet.' Hence the images of the one are drawn from the study, those of the other from the field. 'Whatever pathos there is in either results from the recollection of friendship terminated by death.' The comparison of Milton with Cowley is about as unfortunate as any that could have

---

[1] See collection of criticisms in the editions of Warton and Todd. The answer of Professor Masson touching the alleged insincerity of Milton's sorrow is given further on (p. 30).

been made, either as regards true feeling or true poetry. The reader may judge for himself by contrasting the following extract from the elegy on the *Death of Hervey* with any corresponding passage in *Lycidas* he may choose to select:—

> Ye fields of Cambridge, our dear Cambridge, say,
> *Have ye not seen us walking every day?*
> *Was there a tree about*, which did not know
>   The love betwixt us two?
> Henceforth, ye gentle trees, for ever fade,
>   Or your sad branches thicker join,
>   And into darksome shades combine,
> Dark as the grave wherein my friend is laid.

Or again—

> *Wondrous young man*, why wert thou made so good
> To be snatched hence, *ere better understood?* &c. &c.

But enough of this. We know that Dr. Johnson had no genuine appreciation of poetry; yet his shrewd intelligence and the soundness of his judgment on most literary points might have enabled him to write a fairer critique of Milton's early poems, had not the marked opposition of his religious and political principles to those of our author prejudiced his mind against the *man*, and thus prevented his forming an impartial estimate of the *poet*, even where the conflict of their respective opinions was not concerned. Hallam notes it as remarkable that Johnson had before 'selected Virgil's 10th Eclogue for peculiar praise, which belongs to the same class of allegory and requires the same sacrifice of reasoning.' As to the second objection, it may be urged that though Milton has brought together in the same poem heathen and Christian images, he has not grouped them confusedly together, nor united them in action, but dealt with them in proper succession. The passage which treats of the corruption of the clergy in *Lycidas* is as completely isolated as that about the Syrian shepherdess in the *Epitaph on the Marchioness of Winchester*. So in the *Nativity Hymn* the epithet 'Great Pan' is applied to the new-born child, just as our Lord is spoken of as 'Pan,' in Spenser's 5th and 7th eclogues—the sense in which the early Church loved to express such words as those of St. John x. 11, when on the walls of the catacombs the first Christians pictured the Good Shepherd. The mingling of sacred and profane allusions appears in a more glaring form in such passages as Spenser, *F. Q.* I. x. 53, where Mount Sinai and the Mount of Olives are placed with Mount Parnassus; or in Surrey's Translation of Æneid IV., where we have 'holy water stocks' in Dido's temple, and 'nun' commonly used of a pagan priestess (cf. Drayton, Ecl. 5, 'Diana's nuns'); and Shakspere's *Midsummer Night's Dream*, i. 1, where 'nun' and 'cloister' are mentioned along with Diana, Venus, &c. 'Church' is used of heathen temples (cf. Acts xix. 37), e.g. 'Church of Jove' in Marlowe's *Lucan*, and 'Church of Pallas' in Chaucer, who also calls Amphiaraus, priest of Apollo, a 'bishop.' It is therefore unfair to say that Milton is alone and conspicuous in these irregularities. The early Italian poetry also affords frequent instances of the intrusion of strictures on the clergy; the introduction of St. Peter in company with Triton and Neptune reminds us of Dante's making Cato Uticensis porter of Purgatory, and the excuse which has been offered for the one poet may fairly enough be urged for the other—'Per verità è un gran capriccio, ma in ciò segue suo stile.'[1]

The *Lycidas* may therefore be described as an allegoric pastoral representing College life and friendship, and is cast mainly in the form of Greek and Latin pastorals, though the scenery is transferred to the British Isles. Nowhere is the student brought in as such; nor is the pastoral disguise ever dropped, except in the digression upon Fame and in the isolated passage about the clergy where another kind of shepherd appears upon the scene. Virgil's 10th Eclogue is in most points similar, even including those few lines (44–49) in which he describes Gallus as an actual soldier of the camp in Italy.

---

[1] See Neve's *Cursory Remarks on some English Poets* (1789).

INTRODUCTION.

There is really the same confusion in *Lycidas*, though its circumstances are not quite so incongruous. Lycidas, as a shepherd, had no more to do with a shipwreck than Gallus, as a shepherd, with the army; but in the former instance the pastoral fiction passes more easily into the actual circumstances of King's death than in the case of Gallus. The allegory proper extends only to King's life and to Milton's connection with him, while the catastrophe is given as it actually occurred. So in Virgil Lycoris is not represented as an actual shepherdess, but is supposed to have literally gone away to the Alps with a rival. What gives Milton more license in his treatment is the fact that *Lycidas* is not an avowed pastoral, forming one of a series of the same kind; whereas Virgil's 10th Eclogue does occur in such a connexion and cannot well be separated from the rest. Virgil was ostensibly engaged in pastoral compositions and introduced the story of Gallus among them; Milton however not being previously thus occupied, but starting with a desire to celebrate his lost friend's memory, availed himself of a form of poetry which was at the time most in vogue. The opening lines [1] show that Milton had not meant to write verse again until he had attained the full maturity of that poetic power which he had long felt within him; yet the tribute due to his deceased friend overcame this resolution, and thus the expression of his grief is the pervading thought of the whole. It may even be that the fact of King's having been intended for holy orders was the starting point whence sprang those well-known lines on the English clergy which eventually became the most significant part of the poem, and the heading added in 1645 is an express intimation that Milton intended to give special prominence to lines which were originally suggested by his immediate subject, and in fact only came in by way of digression.

There are two such digressions in *Lycidas* (see notes on *ll.* 85 and 132)—one on Fame, the other on the corruptions of the clergy. Touching the first, the consideration of a life

---

[1] See note on 'Once more,' *l.* 1.

of youthful promise, so suddenly cut short, leads to the reflection that after all there may be no use in human labour and striving after fame; but he turns from all this to the lofty truth, that the power of faultless discernment and the final meed of fame are in the hands of an all-wise and supreme Judge. Here Milton has lighted upon a grand fact of humanity which cannot be better expressed than in the words of a recent writer in the *Contemporary Review* (April 1872):—'The desire for fame is the craving to be judged fairly . . . an universal instinct of mankind. Man has a right to a just judgment, which is to be welcomed as a privilege. . . . Real reputation is the reflection of the glory of God upon the lives of men; but when men feel they are not appreciated, they make their appeal to another life, and claim to stand before the eternal judgment-seat.'

The second digression is probably his first definite expression of feeling on Church matters, not as yet decidedly anti-episcopalian. He simply laments the state of things existing; but it was not till 1641 that he directly ascribed it to the influence of prelacy (*Reason of Church Government*). The papists ceased to be troublesome after the death of Mary of Scotland (1587), and the defeat of the Spanish Armada (1588); but now the ultra-Protestant party[1] began to desire an advanced reformation, having already (1563) attacked the vestments and ceremonies of the Reformed Church. Episcopacy was denounced on the ground of not being expressly ordered in Scripture, while government by elders was held to be divinely appointed.[2] In 1593 an Act was passed against Romanists and Puritans equally, for non-acceptance of the Liturgy was made equivalent to

---

[1] Walton (*Life of Hooker*) notices three parties then in England: 'the active Romanists, the restless Nonconformists, and the passive, peaceable Protestants.' The first lost power after the death of Mary; and the second he charges with 'an innate restless pride and malice—opposition to the government and especially to the bishops.'

[2] On this point see remarks of Mr. M. Arnold, in the *Cornhill Magazine* for Feb. 1870, on the difference between the Puritan theory and that of the Established Churches upon Church Government.

disloyalty. This identification by statute soon led to some disaffection, though in Elizabeth's reign the political side of Puritanism did not strongly appear, as all parties felt that their strength was bound up with the safety of her person and her throne.[1] But the character of James I. secured no such esteem; and the Puritans began to assume a more decided antagonism, both political and religious. The Hampton Court Conference (1604) was on the whole unfavourable to their party; the doctrine of the divine right of kings was gratifying to James, and the two maxims—*Le roy s'avisera*, and *No bishop, no king*—went together. The Millenary Petition was rejected, and the 141 Canons[2] enforced conformity with great rigour. The 'King's Letters' of 1623, for restraining extravagant preaching on both sides, fell perhaps more heavily on the Puritans, with whom a lengthy exposition of doctrine was a *sine qua non*, than on the Prelatists who made this a matter of less vital importance, and who were, moreover, content that catechising on the Sunday afternoons should take the place of sermons (see note on *l.* 125). Charles I. (1625) united the pretensions of absolute monarchy with those of a powerful hierarchy, and thus Crown and Church were opposed to People and Puritans. Church and State questions were more closely related than ever; and the influence, first of Buckingham, and then of Strafford and Laud, tended to the same result. The Star Chamber and High Commission Courts went hand in hand; and the resistance of Hampden to an unjust impost was almost coincident with the outcry against the new Liturgy in Scotland. On March 10, 1629, Charles dissolved the parliament, and seemed intent on ruling without one. Now the struggle began in earnest. For some time there had been 'an anti-Calvinistic spirit in the English Church, which was now spreading among the younger clergy' (see Masson's *Life of*

---

[1] See Macaulay, *Hist. of England*, vol. I. ch. i.

[2] The Canons assert Royal Supremacy, Authority of Church Synods, Episcopacy, Established Order of Services, and condemn all impugners of Church order and discipline as hereby established.

Milton, i. p. 309, and also the account of the consecration of St. Katharine Cree Church in Fuller). Laud was Bishop of London, and virtually Primate; the death of Buckingham had given him paramount influence with the king, and the patronage of Church benefices was largely in his hands. He was a man of small intellect, but of great tenacity of purpose; and 'his nature if not great was very tight' (Masson, i. p. 361). All his views centred in divine right of bishops and uniformity in the Church; and he was of opinion that 'unity cannot long continue in the Church when uniformity is shut out at the church-door' (Laud's Diary). In 1633 the period of 'Thorough' began; Wentworth ruled despotically in Ireland, Laud was made Primate, great strictness of Church discipline was enforced, and Prynne was imprisoned for his *Histriomastix*. In 1637 Prynne, Burton, and Bastwick were pilloried, the question of ship-money was decided against Hampden (June 12), a placard designating Laud 'the arch-wolf of Canterbury' was posted at Cheapside,[1] and Williams, Bishop of Lincoln, a friend of the Puritans, was imprisoned (July 11) for alleged libel. On July 23 a tumult arose in Edinburgh about the New Liturgy, which lasted for many weeks, and issued finally in the signing of the New Covenant (Feb. 28 or March 1, 1638). Then the Scotch bishops were deposed, and the Covenanters prepared for war.

As to Milton's own religious sentiments, we know that from his father he inherited strict Puritan principles, yet accompanied with refined æsthetic tastes. His early surroundings were Puritan, and Richard Stock, 'a zealous Puritan,' was pastor of the parish in which he lived. The time of his birth (1608) was that in which the Puritan party was gaining strength, though still in the minority. His early training was under his father (cf. *Epist. ad Patrem*), who doubtless exercised much influence upon his opinions. Next he was under the care of Young, a Puritan minister (*Ep. Fam.* 1. El. 4), and afterwards at St.

[1] See beginning of Appendix II.

Paul's School, under the two Gills (*Ep. Fam.* 2, 3, 5). His reading was very wide, including, besides the classics, French, Italian, Hebrew, and the mass of English literature then existing.[1] His early versions of Psalms cxiv. and cxxxvi. show extensive reading. In February 1625 he entered Cambridge, where there was a strong Puritan element, Dr. Preston of Emanuel being the leader. Christ's College was less impregnated with these principles, and Chappell himself was in Laud's interest, who afterwards made him Bishop of Cork. The Latin elegies on Bishops Andrewes and Felton (1626) show that Milton was not then an anti-Prelatist, and the Ode *in Quintum Novembris* of the same year is laudatory of the 'pious James.' In 1627 his Elegy to Young, who had fled to Hamburg probably because of his non-conformity, expresses affection for him and sympathy with his doctrines. In July 1628 he writes to A. Gill, deploring the ignorance of the clergy; and in the same year he wrote the Academic *Prolusion* on 'the compatibility of sportive exercise with the study of philosophy' (Masson, i. p. 250 foll.), which contains specimens of outrageous license and even of coarse obscenity, for which, however, he apologises on the ground of long-standing custom. He there designates the students generally as 'calf-heads,' 'rams,' 'Irish birds,' &c. &c., and by other titles quite unmentionable; all which shows that he could at times throw off his habitual seriousness. The general idea we gather of Milton's University life is that he was serious and earnest, reading with unusual vigour, but, being thrown among companions for the most part uncongenial, he had little affection for the place.[2] In the *Apol. Smect.* (1642)

---

[1] The chief authors Milton probably read are—Chaucer (ending 1400), Lydgate, Ascham, Skelton, Surrey, Wyatt, &c. (1400-1580); and the Elizabethans (1580-1625) Sidney, Hooker, Raleigh, Bacon, Spenser, Sackville, Daniel, Drayton, Chapman, Sylvester's *Du Bartas*, Donne, Davies, the two Fletchers, Wither, Carew, Browne, Greene, Marlowe, Shakspere, Heywood, Ben Jonson, Beaumont and Fletcher, Massinger and Ford.

[2] See 1st Elegy (to Diodati): 'Quam male Phœbicolis convenit ille locus;' also in his letter to Gill (1624) he writes: 'Atque ego profecto *cum nullos fere studiorum consortes hic reperiam*, Londinum recta respicerem, nisi per justitium hoc

he says of the University—'In the time of her better health and mine own younger judgment I never greatly admired (her), so now much less.'

In 1629 he took his B.A., and subscribed the Articles (a ceremony which he repeated in 1632 on taking his M.A.); and in the same year he wrote his 6th Elegy to Diodati, in praise of wine and mirth, though he says that the higher poesy demands pure life and spare living. The *Nativity Ode* contains a decided opinion in favour of Church music, and this is expressed again in the ode *At a Solemn Musick* and towards the end of the *Penseroso*; but in the later treatise on *Christian Doctrine*, bk. ii. c. 4, he inveighs against all external worship, quoting Amos vi. 5, 'Woe to them...that chaunt to the sound of the viol,' &c.

In a letter to a friend, December 1631, inclosing the 7th sonnet, he declares his unwillingness to take holy orders, chiefly on the ground of unfitness; but in the *Reason of Church Government* (1641) he stated his objections more clearly thus— 'I thought it better to prefer a blameless silence before the sacred office of speaking, bought and begun with servitude and forswearing.' *L'Allegro* and *Il Penseroso*, written in or near 1632, are both far from Puritanical—the one being a joyous outburst of mirth and fancy, free from the least sensuous taint, and the other expressing the melancholy of a studious mood without sourness or austerity. The Masques of *Arcades* and *Comus* (1634) represent a kind of amusement which he afterwards, in his *Free Commonwealth*, disapproved because of its licentiousness. But *Comus* is itself a protest against this very thing, and thereby, instead of inveighing at the immorality of the stage after the usual Puritanical manner, he showed practically how to turn such things to good account.

By birth and education then Milton was in every respect a Puritan, notwithstanding his classical learning and his genuine

æstivum (*the Long Vacation*) in otium alte literarium recedere cogi- tarem, et quasi claustris musarum delitescere.' (See note on *l.* 34.)

love for the beautiful. He was a man of few convictions, but these were strong and lasting, the uppermost feeling of his mind being that a ceaseless and determined struggle must be maintained against the evil that is in the world. In both his prose and his poetry *liberty* stands forth as the ideal ; and this yearning after freedom fostered in him a resolute dislike of that religious and civil formality, which had displaced the healthy and genial life of the preceding Elizabethan times. Moreover the impulse of an indwelling poetic life, and an exalted idea of human duties and responsibilities, 'as ever underneath the great Taskmaster's eye,' would often bear him beyond the narrow range of party conflict. His mission was to be a poet first, and a statesman or theologian afterwards. He had also a power of foresight and of self-discipline, which imparted a kind of set purpose to all his works, and caused an absence of those 'strains of unpremeditated art,' which he was himself foremost to appreciate in Shakspere.[1] All along he seems to have consciously nursed his inborn powers, unwilling before the full growth of his genius to begin the lofty poetic task of which he felt himself capable, 'though of highest hope and hardest attempting.'

It may be that the self-consciousness of the student ever accompanying the poet in Milton has produced an artificial semblance in some of his poetry which may reasonably lead to the question—'How far is *Lycidas* an expression of genuine sorrow?'

In reply to Dr. Johnson's coarse criticism, that it is 'not the effusion of real passion, which runs not after remote allusions and obscure opinions,' that 'where there is leisure for fiction there is little grief,' that 'there is no nature, for there is no truth,' and that 'no image of tenderness can be excited by the lines "we drove afield,"' &c.—the opinions of some other critics have already been quoted,[2] to which may be added

---

[1] *L'Allegro*, 133—
'And sweetest Shakspere, Fancy's child,

Warble his native wood-notes wild.'

[2] See p. 20.

Hallam's remark (*Hist. of Eng. Lit.* vol. iii. p. 46), that 'it has been said fairly that *Lycidas* is a good test of real feeling in poetry.' But no better or more comprehensive answer could be given than the following, which we take the liberty of quoting from Masson's *Life of Milton*, vol. iii. p. 84: It is 'a finer monument to the memory of King—to let the fact of his death originate a whole mood of the poet's mind—than if he had merely registered the fact in a lyric of direct regret. So poets honour the dead: they let his image intertwine itself with all else that arises in their minds; and out of the best choosing still the best, they lay *that* on the tomb, saying, " This belongs to *you*."'[1] Yet Dr. Johnson, notwithstanding his prejudice, forgot certain facts which he might with a little ingenuity have pressed into his service. First, we know nothing whatever of Milton's relations with Edward King, except what we gather from this poem. There is no mention of any kind of association between them during their college career. Secondly, we do know that King gained the fellowship over Milton's head; and thirdly, Milton does not notice King's death to Diodati, though writing only a month afterwards. As to the disappointment about the fellowship, we have no right to suppose that it led to any coldness between the two friends, and it would not have been like Milton to allow this. The first and third points are purely negative, so that after all we must look to the *Lycidas* to speak for itself. The mere form of the poem can prove nothing against the genuineness of Milton's regret, for grief, like all deep feeling, will reflect the tendency or mental habit of the patient. Thus Cicero philosophised grief when his daughter died; and Marmontel, the dramatist, wrote the play of *Penelope* on the death of his child; to which we may add the example of our own poet laureate in his exquisite *In*

---

[1] Of the *Lycidas* it may be truly said (to use the language of one of our public journals), that it is not to be classed among 'the coldly-correct Jeremiads, in which at the grave of academical renown rhetorical tears are shed with artistic precision and griefs meted out in strict accordance with the canons of the schools.'—*Daily Telegraph*, on death of Charles Dickens, June 20, 1870.

Memoriam. It was, therefore, only natural that Milton should give vent to his grief in verse, and in that kind of verse which was then most usual on such occasions. But we must be careful lest the pathos and intrinsic beauty of much of the poem should lead us into an exaggerated idea of the extent of his sorrow. We may safely conclude with Professor Masson that King was really a friend, but not *the* friend of his youth. For both the evidence of Milton's correspondence with Diodati, and the intense and passionate grief of some portions of the *Epitaphium Damonis*, prove that he and not King was deepest in his affections. Yet the elegy in which he laments the loss of Diodati is a pastoral, cast in a form more artificial than even the *Lycidas*, and written not in English but in Latin. We will now proceed to give some account of this other poem.

The subject of it, Charles Diodati (see the Argument), was born in 1608, and was therefore about the same age as Milton. His father, Theodore Diodati, was an Italian by descent, but married an English lady of good fortune, and was appointed physician to Prince Henry and the Princess Elizabeth, afterwards Queen of Bohemia: his uncle, Giovanni Diodati, was the author of the Italian translation of the Bible, known by his name. He formed a close intimacy with Milton at St. Paul's School, which he left in 1621 for Trinity College, Oxford, where Alexander Gill, son of the head-master of St. Paul's, had also been educated. The friendship between the two young men continued throughout their university career, though they could only meet in London during the vacations, and correspond by letters at other times. Two of Diodati's epistles are extant, written in Greek, probably in 1625 and 1626, and bearing the headings Θεόσδοτυς Μίλτωνι εὐφραίνεσθαι and χαίρειν respectively. The first name is, of course, a literal rendering of the Italian *Dio-dāti*, 'God-given' (see note on *Epit. Dam.* 210). To this letter Milton appears to have replied in the elegiac poem which stands first in the collection entitled *Elegiarum Liber*, the third line of which shows that his friend was then residing in Cheshire, somewhere on the banks of the Dee.

From the heading prefixed to the 6th elegy of the same series we learn that Diodati had on Dec. 15, 1629, sent Milton a copy of verses, describing the Christmas festivities he was then enjoying, and pleading these by way of excuse if his poetry were found to be 'less good than usual' ('sua carmina excusari postulasset, si solito minus essent bona'). Milton's answer is that conviviality and poetry, 'Bacchus and the Muse,' are not hostile to one another, but go well in company; only that he who would sing of high and holy themes, ' of heaven and pious heroes and leaders half divine'—*he* must live soberly and severely, with chaste morals and stainless hands. The elegy concludes with a mention of the Hymn on Christ's Nativity, upon which the poet was at that time engaged, and which he promises to submit to his friend for criticism (see on *Epit. Dam.* 180).

After this we have no more direct information about Diodati until Sept. 2, 1637, when Milton addressed to him a Latin epistle, complaining of his long silence, and expressing a hope that they might shortly meet in London. From this and the following letter (dated Sept. 23 of the same year) we gather that Diodati was now in full medical practice, probably in Cheshire,—'among the Hyperboreans,' as Milton jocosely terms the natives of those parts,—that he made occasional journeys for visiting and recreation, and that he had a regular lodging in town, where Milton once expected to find him, but was disappointed. Part of the second letter will presently be quoted (in translation) in the note on *l.* 150 of the *Epitaphium*; and towards the end of it Milton intimates his intention of taking chambers in one of the Inns of Court for the purpose of study; but this plan appears to have been abandoned in favour of the continental tour which took place early in the following year (Masson, vol. i. p. 601). It was during this journey (in the summer or autumn of 1638) that Diodati died suddenly. The place and circumstances of his death are alike uncertain; but we know that the sad news did not reach Milton till some time afterwards, as the third Italian sonnet (beginning *Diodati, e te'l dirò con maraviglia*) must have been addressed to his friend from Italy about, or more probably after, the actual time of his decease (ib. p. 775). Prof. Masson argues very plausibly that Milton heard the tidings first from John Diodati, Theological Professor at Geneva, with whom he was staying in June 1639, on his way back to England. But however this may have been, we are sure that grief for the loss of so dear a friend possessed the poet's mind to the temporary exclusion even of those political anxieties which had been the cause of his sudden return. Of this we have evidence not only in the *Epitaphium Damonis* itself, which, notwithstanding its artificial form and its pastoral conceits, is as true an outburst of the bitterest sorrow as anything of the kind we know, but also in Milton's own words forming part of a letter in 1647 to Carlo Dati, one of his former friends at Florence (*Epit. Dam.* 137). After recalling the recollection of their former intimacy, and assuring Dati of his continued affection, he suddenly refers to the memory of the deceased Diodati, and to the grief he had felt at his death, which only the thought of the unmixed joy he had tasted in the society of his Florentine companions could in any way alleviate. We give the extract:—' Testor illum mihi semper sacrum et solenne futurum Damonis tumulum, in cujus funere ornando cum luctu et moerore oppressus, ad ea quæ potui solatia confugere cupiebam, non aliud mihi quicquam jucundius occurrit quam vestrum omnium gratissimam mihi memoriam revocasse. Id quod ipse jamdiu legisse debes, siquidem ad vos illud carmen pervenit, quod ex te nunc primum audio.' The 'carmen' referred to is in fact the *Epitaphium Damonis*, a copy of which Milton had sent to Dati as a token of his regard, on account of his name being mentioned therein (137 l. c.).

Of the poem itself we have already spoken incidentally in our observations on the *Lycidas*, and much of what has been said of the one applies with equal force to the other. It is, however, more of a direct and avowed pastoral, and was evidently suggested by the Ἐπιτάφιος Βίωνος of Moschus, whence its title is taken. We have had occasion to mention and partly to examine that poem as a specimen of Greek pastoral (see p. 5), and we then noticed how the real circumstances of the life and death of Bion appear from time to time through the veil of allegory under which the poet has chosen to disguise his personality. The same fact is observable in several passages of Milton's *Epitaphium*, in which the poet's actual self is blended with the character of the ideal Thyrsis, and the person of the real Diodati with that of the shepherd Damon. Nor is this surprising; the image of his lost friend was too vividly impressed upon Milton's soul, and his grief (like that of Moschus for Bion) too sincere to allow him to sustain with absolute continuity his assumed disguise, which, be it remembered, he had adopted merely in deference to the then prevailing fashion, and would not, even on purely critical grounds, have felt himself bound to keep with undeviating precision. Yet he never allows this liberty to degenerate into a license: the strain of the poem is pastoral throughout—far more so than in the case of the *Lycidas*, whose variations and digressions have already been discussed in detail. It is this very freedom of treatment which gives the *Epitaphium Damonis* its real value and interest, claiming for it recognition as a record of one period in the life of a great and distinguished man, about which we should otherwise have had but scanty information. The following remarks by Warton, in answer to some rather disparaging criticism of Dr. Johnson on this poem, are very much to the point: 'The pastoral form is a fault of the poet's times.' The poem 'contains some passages which wander far beyond the bounds of bucolick song, and are in his own original style of the more sublime poetry. Milton cannot be a shepherd long. His native powers often break forth, and cannot bear the assumed disguise.' We subjoin a list of those passages, in which the pastoral allegory is for the moment abandoned.

In *l.* 13, Thyrsis is described as sojourning *Tusca in urbe*, i.e. at Florence, where Milton was actually staying at the time for literary purposes—'animi causa' as the Argument expresses it. As a shepherd he would have no business there, so far away from home and for such an object.

Ll. 46–49 may be applied either way, but seem to convey the idea of a student's rather than of a shepherd's fireside.

The 'Attic salt' of *l.* 56 admits of only one application.

Ll. 113 foll. describe Milton's actual journey to Italy, which has nothing to do with his assumed pastoral character. (Compare the parallel instance of Gallus, in Virgil's 10th Eclogue, see p. 23 of this Introduction.)

In *ll.* 126–138 the accidental circumstance of Diodati's Tuscan origin is mentioned in the middle of an imaginary description of Tuscan swains, among whom the actual names of Dati and Francini occur, not under a classical designation (like Lycidas and Menalcas, *l.* 132), but just slightly Latinised.

Ll. 162–178. Here the poet is confused with the shepherd—the intention of the real Milton to write a real British epic being stated partly in plain language, partly under a pastoral figure (168–171).

L. 181. The name of Manso, Milton's Neapolitan host, is introduced with scarcely any disguise, and the description of the chased goblets which follows, though probably real (see note *ad loc.*), is at any rate not drawn from the circumstances of bucolic life.

Ll. 209–219. The pastoral imagery now entirely disappears; the name Diodatus is substituted for that of Damon, and his present state of bliss among the saints in heaven is described in Scriptural language, which is in the last line curiously varied by a Pagan but not distinctively pastoral metaphor—' bacchantur '—' orgia '—' thyrso.'

The scene is laid in England, as appears from the mention of the Chelmer (*l.* 90 note) and of the Colne (*l.* 149), but the associations are necessarily classical, owing to the form in which the poem is cast. Those who adopt what we have endeavoured to represent as the right view of the requirements of a modern pastoral will not blame Milton for this; but will transfer their censure to the Roman poet, who by blending Sicilian with Italian scenery originated the confusion. Still the introduction of lions and wolves in *ll.* 41, 42 would better have been avoided, though a similar mistake is made by Virgil in his 5th Eclogue (*l.* 26) without equal excuse for it.

The *Epitaphium Damonis* has been rendered into English by Symmons (about 1804) in the Life of Milton appended to his edition of the Prose Works; also by Langhorne (1760), as far as *l.* 138; and again by Cowper. A new translation into English hexameters is given by Professor Masson, in the second volume of his *Life of Milton*, which, by the courtesy of the author, I am enabled to reprint entire.

Of detached pieces of criticism on the *Lycidas* the following are given by Todd in his edition of Milton's poetical works:—

1. Peck's *Explanatory and Critical Notes, &c.*, printed with his *New Memoirs of Milton* (1740).
2. Remarks in Dr. Johnson's *Lives of the Poets* (Life of Milton) (1781).
3. *Critical Essay on Lycidas* by John Scott (1785).
4. *Cursory Remarks on some ancient English Poets, particularly Milton*, by P. Neve (1789). To these we need only add the complete account and examination of this poem and the *Epitaphium Damonis* in vols. i. and ii. of Professor Masson's *Life of Milton* (1859 and 1871).

The *Lycidas* was translated into Latin by William Hogg (Hogæus) in 1694, and into Greek by Plumptre, Canon of Worcester, in 1797. Both these translations have been made use of in the notes to this edition; the former is reprinted at the end of the volume.

As might be expected, the poem has found many imitators. The first 'imitations, or rather open plagiarisms from Milton' (as Warton says), were made in 1647 by Robert Baron in a poetical romance, entitled the *Cyprian Academy* (see Todd, Appendix to vol. vi.). Into this he transferred whole lines and phrases from nearly all Milton's early poems, then lately published; and from *Lycidas* was borrowed the greater part of the floral description in *ll*. 135–151. Samuel Boyse, in his *Vision of Patience* (1741), laments the death of a Mr. Cumming, lost at sea, under the name 'Lycidas,' but does not otherwise imitate Milton's monody. In 1760 Robert Lloyd published the *Tears and Triumph of Parnassus*, containing an ode on the death of the king (George II.), in which occur the lines we have quoted on *l.* 75, beginning, 'Where were the Muses,' &c. In the same note reference is made to a similar passage from Lord Lyttleton's monody on the death of his wife. Michael Bruce, in *Daphnis* (a monody on Mr. Arnot), has these lines:—

> So may I snatch his lays, who to the lyre
> Wailed his lost Lycidas by wood and rill, &c. ;

and further on—

> *Where were the Muses*, when the leaden hand
> Of death remorseless closed your Daphnis' eyes?
>   Fair was thy thread of life,
> But quickly *by the envious sisters shorn;*
> So Daphnis died, long *ere his prime* he fell,
> Nor *left he* on these plains *a peer* behind.

The metre is arranged in long and short lines at irregular intervals, like those in the *Lycidas*. We may also notice a monody on the death of Queen Adelaide by Julian Fane, among the Cambridge Prize Poems for 1850, which is closely modelled (as the heading intimates) upon that of Milton. A few extracts are subjoined as examples of the imitation:—

> For she no more upon the dawning day
>   *Listening their joyous lay,*
> Shall bend her wistful eyes for ever closed . . . .
> *Where were ye nymphs* upon that fatal morn? . . . .
> *Alas, what boots it* to enquire your place?
> *For what could ye have done?* . . . .
> Last reverend Camus, as he footed slow, &c.

Besides these and more of the same kind, we have detached

expressions *undique decerpta*, such as 'melt with ruth,' 'but not the wise,' &c. (speaking of Care tormenting the great and proud), 'hence with the blazing clarion of renown' (cf. *Lyc.* 18, and for the sentiment 76 foll.), &c. The monody ends with an apotheosis of the queen which nearly resembles that of *Lycidas*—'Cease, Albion, cease to weep,' 'She shall arise,' &c., 'Now Albion weeps no more,' &c. The latest reminiscence appears in the *London Lyrics* by Mr. Locker (1872):—

> And still the woodland rings, and still
> The old Damœtas listens—

speaking of the youthful glow of life as compared to a laughing leaping rill.

Among the various editions of Milton's poems, which include the *Lycidas*, we select the following:

1. The *Cambridge Verses* of 1638, already referred to (p. 2). The English poems succeed the Latin, and are separately entitled *Obsequies to the Memorie of Mr. Edward King, Anno Domini* 1638.' The *Lycidas* is dated J. M., November 1637, in the MS. preserved in the library of Trinity College, Cambridge. It has no title in this first edition.

2. *Poems of Mr. John Milton, both English and Latin, composed at several times*, collected and republished in 1645. Here the heading, 'In this Monody,' &c., is for the first time prefixed.

3. *Poems, &c., upon several Occasions* (1673, the year before Milton died). This is a reprint of the former, with some additions, and containing the Hartlib Tractate on Education.

4. Successive editions for Tonson (1695–1747).

5. Baskerville's *Poetical Works of Milton* (1758–1760).

6. Newton's editions (1752–1790). Of these Keightley observes in his own preface that they are 'the first English instance of a *Variorum* edition, from MS. notes by Jortin, Warburton, Thyer, Peck, Sympson, &c. Very respectable for those times, when criticism was imperfect, and knowledge of earlier English literature and language slender.'

7. Warton's editions of the smaller poems, except the *Paradise Regained*, with notes (1785 and 1791).

8. Hayley's *Poetical Works of Milton* (1794-1797).

9. Todd's *Poetical Works, &c., with the Principal Notes of various Commentators* (1801, 1809, 1826). Here the substance of Warton's notes is reproduced, with many additions by the editor; they consist of a mass of materials, for the most part undigested and ill-arranged, and are chiefly useful for their collection of parallel passages, though these (as Masson truly remarks, vol. i. p. 534) 'are pushed to the verge of the ridiculous—interesting only as illustrations of similarity of thought and expression among poets of a particular age.'

10. Keightley's *Poetical Works*, &c. (1859). The poems are arranged chronologically, the spelling is modernised, except in the case of a few words, such as 'sovran,' 'highth,' &c., and the punctuation carefully amended. There are no introductions to the separate pieces, the references in the notes are given with the initials of those editors who first observed them, though many of these, as Keightley tells us in his preface, were noticed by himself independently. For the notes he claims the especial merit of terseness and compression, and consequently fails to give us the arguments on both sides in many disputed passages, presenting merely his own conclusions or those of others, without examination in detail, and often without any reasons whatever.

11. *English Poems by John Milton*, edited by R. C. Browne, King's College, London (1870). This edition comprises much useful information within a small space, but does not profess to enter upon a detailed investigation of mooted points. The introduction has a great deal of original matter, well considered and clearly expressed. The editor frequently adopts the conclusions of Mr. Keightley, to whom he specially acknowledges his obligation in a short preface prefixed to the notes.

A new and complete edition of Milton is promised by Professor Masson, and is expected shortly to appear.[1]

[1] See Preface to Second Edition.

The original MS. of *Lycidas* (together with those of the *Arcades*, *Comus*, and some of the minor poems) is preserved in the library of Trin. Coll., Cambridge. These were collected by Charles Mason and Thomas Clark, Fellows of Trinity, in 1736, having been found among MSS. formerly given to the College by Sir H. Newton Puckering, who was educated there, and who died in 1700 (Masson, vol. ii. p. 104). From them Todd in 1801 collected his various readings in the three poems above mentioned; but as his copy of them is not quite accurate, we append the following corrected list :—

l. 10. 'Who would not sing for Lycidas? he *well* knew.'
22. '*To* bid faire peace,' &c. (*To* erased and *And* substituted.)
26. *Glimmering* corrected to *opening.*
30. 'Oft till the ev'n starre bright,' (altered to *that rose in Ev'ning bright.*)
31. 'his *burnisht* weele,' (altered to *westring weele.*)
47. 'Their gay *buttons* weare.' (*beare* is then written and erased, and *wardrope weare* substituted.)
51. 'yor (*your* erased) lov'd Lycidas.'
58. 'What could the *golden-hayrd Calliope*
   For her inchaunting son,
   When shee beheld (*the gods farre sighted bee*)
   His goarie *scalpe rowle downe the Thracian lee.*'

After *l.* 59 is written in the margin—
'Whome universal nature *might* lament,
And heaven and hel deplore,
When his *divine head* downe the streame was sent.'
(*Head* is first altered to *visage*, and then *divine* to *goarie.*)

69. '*Hid in* the tangles,' (changed to *Or with*, &c.)
85. '.... thou *smooth* flood,' (altered to *fam'd*, and then to *honour'd.*) '*Soft*-sliding Mincius,' (altered to *smooth-sliding.*)
105. '*Scraul'd ore* with figures dim,' (changed to *Inwrought.*)
110. '*Tow* massy keys,' &c. (also '*tow*-handed' in *l.* 130.)
114. '*Anough* of such,' &c.
129. '.... *little* sed.' (*nothing* is first written, but erased.)
138. '.... *stintly* (?) looks.' (First *sparely*, which is erased and then replaced.)

INTRODUCTION. 41

The first correction is obscured by the tail of the *p* in the superscribed *sparely* coming down in front of the first letter (which may be either *f* or *ſ*). Mr. Aldis Wright, to whose courtesy I am indebted for these amended readings, believes the word to be *faintly* and not *stintly*.

l. 139. '*Bring* hither,' &c., (corrected to *Throw hither*, &c.)
142 foll. originally stood thus :—
> 'Bring the rathe primrose that *unwedded* dies,
> Colouring the pale cheeke of uninjoyd love,
> And that sad floure that strove
> To write his own woes on the vermeil graine;
> Next adde Narcissus yt still weeps in vaine,
> The *woodbine* and ye pancie freakt wth jet,
> The glowing violet.'

Afterwards Milton inserted *the garish columbine*, but altered it to *the well attir'd woodbine*.

> '*The cowslip* wan that *hangs his* pensive head,
> And every bud that *sorrows liverie* weares.'
>   (First changed to *sad escutcheon beares*, then to *imbroidrie*, and *beares* to *weares*.)
> '*Let* Daffadillies fille thire cups with teares,
> Bid Amaranthus all his beautie shed.'

(These two lines were transposed, and the *let* was altered to *and*.) The whole of the above passage is struck through with the pen, and the substituted lines are written below.

l. 153. 'Let our *sad* thoughts,' &c., (changed to *fraile*.)
154. '. . . . Ye *floods*,' &c., (changed to *shoars*.)
160. '. . . . *Corineus* old.' (*Bellerus* substituted.)
176. '*Listening* the unexpressive nuptial song,' (altered to *and heares*, &c.)

The unsettled state of orthography [1] in Milton's time makes

---

[1] In an article on English orthography in the *Philological Museum*, the writer remarks that the uniform system now in vogue came in about the middle of the 17th century; that it was settled by those who were more or less ignorant of the antecedents of our language, and maintained by compositors, by whose influence certain modes of spelling

it unnecessary to notice in detail the varieties of spelling which occur in various editions of this poem. We shall presently (on *l.* 129) remark upon *sed* and *blew* (*l.* 192) as illustrating the habit of writing to suit the eye as well as the ear; in *l.* 130 *doore* is changed to *dore* in the MS. to coincide with *more* in the next line. For those who are curious in such matters we append a few selected words from the four editions of 1638, 1645, 1673, and 1695 (Tonson's), from which it will be seen that in many instances the earlier ones had the modern orthography, which afterwards got altered; but this is purely accidental.

	1638	1645	1673	1695
l. 37	gone	gon	gon	gon
47	wardrobe	wardrop	wardrop	wardrobe
53	lie	ly	ly	ly
57	been	bin	bin	bin
82	perfect witnesse	perfet witnes	perfet witnes	perfect witness
112	mitred	miter'd	miter'd	miter'd
114	enough	anow	anow	anow
128	wolf	woolf	woolf	woolf
129	said	sed	sed	sed
140	turf	terf	terf	'terf
175	oazie locks	oozy Lock's	oozy Lock's	oozy Locks
185	perillous	perilous	perilous	perillous
186	oaks	Okes	Okes	Okes
192	blew	blew	blew	blew

In Milton's MS. the preterites and past participles in *-ed* are almost uniformly spelt with the apostrophe, as *destin'd*, *honour'd*, &c.; even *mitre'd* is thus given, where no vowel is omitted. *Honied* seems to be the only instance in *Lycidas* to the contrary. The forms in *-t* are sometimes with and sometimes without the apostrophe, as *nurs't*, *danc't*, &c., by the

became established as the general usage. He further observes that no usage can make a blunder right, and that the right spelling is that which agrees best with pronunciation, etymology, and the analogy of a word to others of the same class to which it belongs.

side of *askt*, *freakt*, &c. It should be noted that the use of the apostrophe began nearly about Milton's time, and continued to be usual till quite lately. Spenser very seldom employs it; he generally omits the *e* altogether, as *joyd*, *cloyd*, &c., sometimes placing it at the end, as *spide*, *obeyde*, &c. After *k*, *n*, *p*, *s*, &c., the letter *t* is used, as *pluckt*, *learnt*, *topt*, *tost*, *pusht*, some of which forms are still to be met with. Originally, as in Chaucer, whenever *-ed* was written, it was meant to be sounded; hence arose these various contrivances to show when it was mute.

Lycidas is the last poem, excepting the *Sonnets*, which Milton wrote in rime. In the preface, added in 1668 to *Paradise Lost*, he speaks of 'rime' as being nothing but 'the invention of a barbarous age to set off wretched matter and lame metre,' and congratulates himself upon having in that poem set the first example in English ' of ancient liberty recovered to heroic poem from the troublesome and modern bondage of riming.' Yet the skilful arrangement of rimes in *Lycidas*, and the exquisite cadences which his fine musical ear enabled him to produce, without rule and apparently without effort, are an evidence of how much may be done by means of an expedient which he afterwards so unsparingly denounced; and there is perhaps no poem which exhibits these qualities in equal profusion. The idea of the system, in which the rimes occur sometimes alternately, but more often at longer and irregular intervals, the ten-syllabled lines being now and then varied by shorter ones of six syllables, is derived from the Italians. The following extracts from choruses in Tasso's *Aminta* and Guarini's *Pastor Fido* will show what the originals were like, but it will be seen that Milton has made considerable variations upon his models.

1. From *Aminta*, Act iv. Scene 2 :—

> Ciò che morte rallenta, Amor, restringi,
> Amico tu di pace, ella di guerra;

E del suo trionfar trionfi e regni,
E mentre due bell' alme annodi e cingi,
Così rendi sembiante al ciel la terra,
Che d' abitarla tu non fuggi o sdegni.
Non son vie là su ; gli umani ingegni
Tu placidi ne rendi, e l' odio interno
Sgombri, signor, da' mansueti cori,
Sgombri mille furori,
E quasi fai col tuo valor superno
Delle cose mortali un giro eterno.

2. From *Pastor Fido*, Act iv. Scene 9 :—

O béllạ età dell' oro,
Quand' éra cíbo il látte
Del párgoletto móndo, e cúlla il bósco
E i cári párti lóro
Godeàn le grégge intátte,
Nè temea 'l mondo ancor ferro nè tosco.
Pensier torbido e fosco
Allór non facēa vélo
Al sól di lúce etérna
Or là ragion, che vérna
Tra le nubi del sénso, ha chiúso il cielo.
Ond' è che 'l péregríno
Va l' áltrui térra, e 'l már turbándo il píno.

Peck, in his *New Memoirs of Milton* (1740), fancifully compares the *Lycidas* to a piece of music, consisting of so many bars, which are represented by the paragraphs ; each rime being a *chord*, and the lines without any answering rime being *discords*. He cites the Pindaric odes of Cowley as examples of similar irregularity in riming, only that in these there are no discords or lines without rimes. The distinction between 'chords' and 'discords' (as if they were two different things in music) is of course erroneous ; but, substituting *phrases* for 'bars' and *concords* for 'chords' in the above comparison, we may allow that the effect upon the ear of an occasional unrimed line bears some analogy to that produced by an unresolved discord in harmony. Nevertheless so artistic is the whole metrical arrangement of this charming monody that the sensations experienced by the most fastidious reader can never be otherwise than agreeable, and to the judgment of such we confidently leave the decision of the question, whether (as Dr. Johnson will have it) 'the diction is harsh, the rhymes uncertain, and the numbers unpleasing.'

LYCIDAS.

YET once more, O ye laurels, and once more
Ye myrtles brown, with ivy never sere,

1] '**Once more**, amid my various occupations, do I return to poetry, that I may offer a tribute to the memory of my deceased friend.' It seems better to understand the allusion thus than to restrict it (as Peck and Newton have done) to 'poems on like occasions' with that of the *Lycidas*, such as the *Ode on the Death of a Fair Infant*, the *Epitaph on the Marchioness of Winchester*, and the four Latin Elegies of 1626. Since the production of *Comus* in 1634, the poet's pen had been unemployed, and we know from his letter to Diodati of Sept. 23, 1637, that he was now studying ancient and mediæval history, in preparation for his Italian tour, which took place in the following spring. Warton properly observes that the plants specified in this and the next line are not peculiar to elegy, but 'symbolical of general poetry.' As evergreens they are also emblems of immortality, which is perhaps the leading idea intended to be conveyed. Cf. Drayton, 6th *Pastoral Eclogue*:—

'Nor mournful cypress nor sad widowing yew
About thy tomb to prosper shall be seen;

But *bay and myrtle*, which is ever new,
In spight of winter flourishing and green.'

There seems to be no sufficient ground for the distinction which Newton draws between the laurel, myrtle, and ivy, as representing the poetic talent of the deceased, his ripeness for love, and his learning (Hor. *Od.* I. i. 29) respectively. Drayton, however, in his 3rd Eclogue, speaks of 'bays that poets do adorn, And myrtle of chaste lovers worn.'

2 **brown**] dark and sombre (It. *bruno*); the *pulla myrtus* of Hor. *Od.* I. xxv. 18.

ivy never sere] Cf. Sylvester, *Du' Bartas*, 70, 'immortal bays never unleaved.' **Sere** (O. E. *seár*, verb *sedrian*) occurs only twice elsewhere in Milton, *P. L.* x. 1071 and *Psalm* ii. 27. Cf. *Macbeth*, v. 3, 'the sear the yellow leaf;' Spenser, *Ecl.* i. 37, 'My lustfull leaf is dry and sere,' where it is explained in the Glossary as an antiquated word, like *guerdon*, *forlorn*, and others, which have now returned into use. Newton's statement that 'there are more obsolete words in this than in any other of

I come to pluck your berries harsh and crude,
And with forced fingers rude
Shatter your leaves before the mellowing year,   5
Bitter constraint, and sad occasion dear,

Milton's poems' may well be disputed. (See note on *l*. 189.)

3–8] Those who imagine an allusion to the untimely death of Mr. King in the premature gathering of the laurels, &c., seem to overlook the fact that these plants represent, not the lost friend, but the verses offered to his memory. The metaphor by which an early death is compared to the plucking of unripe fruit (as in Cic. *De Senectute*, 'Quasi poma ex arboribus,' &c., quoted by Dunster) has therefore no application here, the reference being obviously to the poet's efforts in verse, which were, in his own opinion, yet 'harsh and crude,' but whose time of maturity a pious duty compelled him to forestall. Six years previously, in the Sonnet written at the age of twenty-three, he had expressed his resolution not to hasten the time of his 'inward ripeness;' and in the accompanying letter he says, 'I take no thought of being late, so it give advantage to be more fit.'

4 forced] i.e. unwilling, as explained in *ll*. 6, 7.

5] Cf. *P. L.* x. 1066. *Shatter* is a modern softening of *scatter*, like *shave* and *scab*, *sharp* and *scarp*, &c.

mellowing] (*mollis*) would strictly apply to fruit, not to leaves or flowers. But the sense probably is, 'before the advancing year, which ripens the fruit, causes your leaves to fall.' Keightley remarks that 'these plants all shed their leaves during the year, but gradually.' Cf. Marlowe, *Tamburlaine*, ii. 1, 'And fall like mellowed fruit with shakes of death.'

6] Plumptre's translation (1797), πικρὰ ἀναγκαία, λυπρὸν χρῆμ' ἀλλὰ ποθεινόν, probably gives the right sense of this line, i.e. an occasion sad in itself, but concerned about a dear object (Spens. *F. Q.* I. i. 53). But *dear* may mean 'important,' from its primary sense of 'costly' (O. E. *deóre*, G. *theuer*), an interpretation which is slightly favoured by the occurrence of the word with the same meaning and connexion in Sidney's *Arcadia*, where Time is addressed as 'the father of occasion-deare.' Hence arose the peculiar use of 'dear' in a sense apparently contradictory to its usual one, as in Shakspere's 'dearest foe,' 'dear peril,' &c., which is to be explained, not (as Horne Tooke supposes) from *derian*, 'to hurt,' but by a natural transition from the original notion of importance into that of strong interest or emotion, whether of love or hatred. (See Dyce's *Glossary to Shakspere*, pp. 119, 120.)

The position of the noun between the two epithets is very common in Milton. Out of numberless instances which occur, Peck quotes *P. L.* v. 3, 'temperate vapours bland;' ix. 1003, 'mortal sin original.' Cf. also *l*. 4 *supra*, *Arcades*, 49, 51, to which may be added 'the two-topt mount divine' of the supposed Miltonic *Epitaph*—an expression which Dean Stanley in his letter to Prof. Morley (Introd. to *King and Commons*, p. xxxii.) pronounced to be 'Milton all over.' This order of words is imitated from the Greek (cf. Hes. *Theog.* 811, χάλκεος οὐδὸς ἀστεμφής; Eur. *Phœn.* 234, νιφόβολον ὄρος ἱρόν). In Latin the adjectives are usually placed together, either with a conjunction, as 'Fatalis incestus*que* judex,' Hor. *Od.*

Compels me to disturb your season due ;
For Lycidas is dead, dead ere his prime,
Young Lycidas, and hath not left his peer.
Who would not sing for Lycidas! he knew   10

III. iii. 19, or without one, as 'domus exilis Plutonia,' Hor. *Od.* I. iv. 17.; 'suavis daedala tellus,' Lucr. i. 7.

7 compels] instead of *compel*, the 'bitter constraint' and 'sad occasion' being so nearly identical as to form one idea. Cf. Hor. *Od.* I. xvii. 12, 'dis pietas mea Et musa cordi *est*.' But, even without any such connexion of meaning, the Elizabethan writers and their immediate successors commonly made the verb agree in number with the nearest preceding noun. Many instances occur in the Bible, e.g. Prov. i. 27 (where Luther's version also has 'Angst und Noth *kommt*'), ib. ii. 6 ; Luke v. 10. Paul Bayne, in one of his *Letters* (circ. 1600), says, 'You will be desirous of knowing how my wife and her place *agreeth*;' Bacon, *Essay on Masques*, observes that 'double masques . . . *addeth* state and variety,' where no singular noun precedes the verb. Even Mr. Tennyson, in a recent volume of Poems, has the construction, 'I should know what God and man *is*.' But many verbs apparently singular are really examples of the Northern plural in *-s*,—e.g. Shakspere, *Coriolanus*, iv. 1, 'fortune's blows . . . *craves* a noble cunning,' &c. &c. James I. constantly uses this form in his letters to Queen Elizabeth, as 'my articles desyr*is*,' 'your subjectis prefer*is*,' &c.

8 ere his prime] Being only twenty-five years old.

9] Milton probably had in his mind Spenser's *Astrophel*, 7, 8. There is a similar repetition of the name, with marked effect, in the ode on *Death of a Fair Infant*,

26. The present line is imitated by Samuel Boyse (1741) in his *Vision of Patience*, 'Young Lycidas the learned and the good.'

peer] i. e. 'equal,' from *par*. Milton has used the word only twice elsewhere in this original sense, in *P. L.* i. 39, v. 812, though he often applies it to the rebel angels as a title of nobility—e.g. 'the grand infernal *peers*,' &c.— which is also its usual meaning in Shakspere. With the present passage cf. P. Fletcher, *Pisc. Ecl.* vi. I, 'A fisher boy that never knew his *peer*;' Cowley, *Death of Hervey*, 'My sweet companion and my gentle *peer.*' This is another of the words (see note on *sere, l.* 2) explained as obsolete in the Glossary to the *Shepheard's Kalendar*; it must have been familiar in the 14th century, as Wicklif, in his translation of Matt. xi. 16, has 'children that crien unto her *peeris*,' i.e. 'fellows.' For the history of the word see Du Cange, *Glossarium*, 's. v. Pares.

10] Peck compares Virg. *E.* x. 3, 'neget quis carmina Gallo?'

he knew to sing] Cf. *Comus*, 87. These and similar expressions are evidently intended as imitations of the Latin and Greek verb-noun infinitive—e.g. *canere* callebat, ᾔδειν ἠπίστατο, &c. In Spenser's *Ruines of Time* occurs the well-known passage—

'Not to have been dipped in Lethe's lake
Could save the son of Thetis *from to die.*'

(Cf. Eur. *Alcestis*, 11, ὃν θανεῖν ἐρρυσάμην.) But this construction is unnecessary and even inaccurate in

Himself to sing, and build the lofty rime,
He must not float upon his watery bier
Unwept, and welter to the parching wind,

English: first, because the infin. in -*ing* (O. E. -*an*) is the real equivalent of the classical phrase; and secondly, because the sign 'to' was properly used with the gerund in -*anne* or -*eune* to denote a purpose. Probably our English poets, not knowing that the form in -*ing* was really an infinitive, and confounding it with the present participle, which it accidentally resembles, thought that the only way of reproducing the Latin and Greek construction was by the use of the sign 'to' with the verb.

How far this estimate of King's poetry is supported by facts we have no adequate means of ascertaining, since only a few copies of his Latin verses are extant (see Masson's *Life of Milton*, vol. i. pp. 603, 604), which show a fair amount of scholarship, but are of no great poetical merit. Milton may here be using the language of exaggeration, or he may have had other and more sufficient grounds for his opinion than such compositions as these would afford.

build the lofty rime] Todd compares Spenser, *Ruines of Rome*, stanza xxiv.—

'To build with levell of my loftie style
That which no handes can ever-
    moie compyle;'

also Eur. *Supp.* 998, ἀοιδὰς ἐπύργωσε, to which we may add Aristoph. *Ranæ*, 1004, πυργώσας ῥήματα σεμνά. The Latin 'condere carmen' (Lucr. v. 2; Hor. *A. P.* 436, *Epist.* I. iii. 24) is probably here imitated; but the original expression does not necessarily contain any metaphor from building, since *condere* simply means

'to put together,' and is therefore applied to any sort of operation which might come under that general notion, such as building, composing, laying in the tomb, &c.; it is moreover used of prose writing as well as of poetry. Gray, *Death of Hoel*, following Milton, has 'build the lofty verse,' and Merrick (circ. 1700), in his *Ode to Fancy*, 'build the rhyme.' *Rime* = 'verse,' as in *P. L.* i. 16. Elsewhere in Milton the word occurs only in the Preface to *Paradise Lost*, where 'rime' is distinguished from blank verse. Since it is there written *rime*, but *rhyme* in *P. L.* i. 16, Bp. Pearson suggested that Milton purposely varied the spelling to signify the difference of meaning. This idea is at any rate not supported by the present passage, since our poet originally wrote *rime* in his MS., though the printed editions of 1638 and 1645 both have *rhyme*. Hence I have adopted in the text what is now known to be the proper orthography. (See Appendix I.)

12 bier] (O. E. *bǽr*, L. *feretrum*), because the waves *bear* the body on their surface. Cf. Fletcher, *Purple Island*, i. 210, 'The dying swan . . . tides on her watrie hearse.'

13 welter] properly 'to roll' (*wal*-low, G. *wal*-tzen, L. *vol*-vo, Gr. εἰλ-ω). It was formerly used in a wider sense than at present. Cf. *Od. Nat.* 124; *P. L.* i. 78; Spens. *Ecl.* vii. 197, 'These wisards welter in wealth's caves.' Keble, *Christian Year* (4th S. after Trinity), speaks of 'the deep weltering flood.' For a very early use of the word see the *King's Quhair*, by James I. of Scotland, 1423, where the *turning* of Fortune's wheel is called 'the sudayn *weltering* of that

Without the meed of some melodious tear.
Begin then, Sisters of the sacred well,
That from beneath the seat of Jove doth spring;
Begin, and somewhat loudly sweep the string.
Hence with denial vain, and coy excuse—
So may some gentle Muse

ilk quhele.' Cf. Pope, *Odyssey*, xiv. 155, 'he welters on the wave.'
   Parching] describes generally the effect of exposure to the weather, and is used of cold as well as of heat, *P. L.* ii. 594, where Newton comp. *Ecclus*. xliii. 21, 'The cold north wind . . . burneth the wilderness.' Cf. Virg. *G.* i. 93, 'Boreæ penetrabile frigus adurat;' Xen. *Anab.* IV. v. 3, where the wintry wind is said $\dot{\alpha}\pi οκαίειν \pi άντα$.
   meed] (O. E. *mēd*, G. *miethe*, akin to $\mu\iota\sigma θ ός$). . Cf. *l*. 84, the only other instance of the word in Milton. Shakspere uses it frequently. Cf. Spens. *F. Q.* II. iii. 10, 'honour virtue's meed;' Browne, *Brit. Past.*, 'baye the learned shepherd's meede.'
   melodious tear] = 'mournful strain;' imitated by Mason in his *Monody on Pope*, 'the loan of some poetick woe.' Cooper, *Tomb of Shakspere*, 'the gurgling notes of her melodious woe;' Shelley, *Adonais*, 'the lorn nightingale Mourns not her mate with such melodious pain.' Hurd comp. Eur. *Suppl.* 454, $δ άκρυα δ' ἑτοιμάζουσι$ (= 'a dirge'). Cf. Virg. *Æn.* ii. 145, 'his lacrimis vitam damus,' i.e. 'to this sorrowful appeal.' In the *Epitaph on the Marchioness of Winchester* Milton speaks of his verses as 'tears of perfect mōan,' and Spenser entitles his elegy on Sir P. Sidney *Tears of the Muses.*
   15] The customary invocation of the Muses is studied from the opening lines of Hesiod's *Theogony*. The 'sacred well' is Aganippe on

Mount Helicon ($ὅρος μέγα τε ζάθεόν τε$), and not, as Keightley supposes, 'a fount of the poet's own creation,' and the 'seat of Jove' is the altar upon the same hill ($βωμὸν ἐρισθενέος Κρονίωνος$). Cf. *Il Penseroso*, 47, 48; Spenser, *Ecl.* iv. 41, where the name of the mountain is transferred to the spring. 'Well' in the sense of a natural fount occurs only here and in *P. L.* xi. 416 (from Psalm xxxvi. 9).
   17 somewhat loudly] i.e. make no uncertain answer to my appeal (see next line). Todd quotes from Drummond's *Elegy on Gustavus Adolphus*—
'Speak it again, and louder louder
     yet;
Else while we hear the sound we
     shall forget
What it delivers.'

   18 coy] (Fr. *coi*, Lat. *quietus*), formerly said of things as well as of persons (*P. L.* iv. 310). Warton instances from the *Apology for Smectymnuus* 'a *coy* flurting style,' i.e. one which deals in quibbling and subterfuge, and thus eludes the grasp of the understanding; also Drayton, *Past. Ecl.* vii., 'these things are all too *coy* (i.e. difficult) for me.' Chaucer, *Romaunt of the Rose*, has the verb *acoie*, 'to caress.' Cf. Turberville (of Jupiter and Danae), 'when he *coyde* the closed nunne in a towre.'
   19 so may, &c.] probably suggested by the 'sic tibi,' &c. of Virg. *Ecl.* x. 4. Cf. *Ecl.* ix. 40; Hor.

With lucky words favour my destined urn, 20
And as he passes turn,
And bid fair peace be to my sable shroud—
For we were nursed upon the self-same hill,

Od. I. iii. 1. The sense is, 'As the Muses enable me to lament my lost friend, *so* may some kindly poet honour my memory when I am dead.' For *Muse* in the sense of 'poet,' cf. Spenser, *Prothalamion*, 159, 'Some brave Muse may sing;' Dryden, *Abs. and Achit.* 1. 'Adriel . . . . himself a Muse;' Chapman, *Hom. Od.* viii. 499, 'This sung the sacred Muse.' Newton's reference to *Sams. Ag.* 973 is not quite apposite, as Fame is there introduced in her proper character as a divinity, though her gender is changed on the poet's own responsibility. There is some awkwardness here in the use of 'muse' for the inspired poet immediately after the invocation of the Muses as the inspirers of the song, but the sense is clear. In an Italian translation by T. Mathias (1812) 'Muse' is properly rendered 'cantor.'

20 **favour**] from *favere* (εὐφημεῖν) in its technical sense. Hor. *Od.* III. i. 2.

my destined urn] i.e. the *tomb* destined for me. For 'urn' in this sense cf. Shaksp. *Cor.* v. 5—

'The most noble corse that ever herald
Did follow to his urn.'

Dyce, *Glossary*, p. 477, quotes from Fortiguerra's *Ricciardetto*, 'aprir la porta dell' urna' (= *tomba*).

22] There seems to be no necessity for rejecting the usual interpretation of 'shroud' in the sense of graveclothes. Dunster indeed observes that it is 'the Miltonic word for harbour, recess, hiding-place,' and takes it here to mean 'tomb;' but as Milton's use of the word (as a noun) is confined to this and three other passages (*Comus*, 147; *Od. Nat.* 218; *P. L.* x. 1068), in all of which the context shows that it is employed metaphorically, these references prove nothing as to its meaning here. It may, however, mean the black pall that covers the coffin. Mallet, in his *William and Margaret*, has the lines—

'And clay-cold was her lily hand
That held her sable shroud,'

but the phrase is probably copied from Milton. Todd's citations from Sylvester are still less to the point, since two of them do not contain the word at all, and in the third it unquestionably means 'dress of mourning,' in its primary acceptation (O. E. *scrud*) of clothes or covering. Cf. Shaksp. *L. Lab. Lost*, v. 2, 'A smock shall be your shroud,' and (for the secondary sense) Ezek. xxxi. 3, 'a cedar with a shadowing shroud.' Pennant, in his *London*, mentions 'a place called the *shrowds*, a covered space on the side of [Paul's] church.'

23] The poem now passes into the pastoral form; the new paragraph should begin at *l.* 25, the present line being connected with *l.* 18, 'I would fain sing for Lycidas, *for* he was my companion, &c.' Masson, *Life of Milton*, p. 611, says, 'The hill is Cambridge, the joint feeding of the flocks is companionship in study, the rural ditties are academic iambics and elegiacs, and old Damœtas is either Mr. Chappell or some more kindly fellow of Christ's' (see on *l.* 36). Among these college poems were the *Elegiacs to T. Young*, 1626; the

Fed the same flock by fountain, shade, and rill.
Together both, ere the high lawns appeared   25
Under the opening eyelids of the Morn,
We drove a-field, and both together heard

Vacation Exercise, 1628; and the *Nativity Ode*, 1629. King's Latin verses have been already noticed (*l.* 10). P. Fletcher, in his 1st *Piscatory Eclogue*, describes his father's early life under a similar allegory drawn from the fisherman's trade :—

'When the raw blossom of my youth was yet
In my first childhood's green enclosure bound,
Of Aquadune I learnt to fold my net . . .
And guide my boat where Thames and Isis heire,
By lowly Eton slides and Windsor proudly faire.

But when my tender youth gan fairly blow,
I changed large Thames for Camus' narrower seas;
There as my years, so skill with years did grow,
And now my pipe the better sort did please;
So that with Limnus and with Belgio
I durst to challenge all my fisher peeres,
That by learn'd Camus' banks did spend their youthfull yeares.'

25 **lawns**] *P. L.* iv. 252; *L'Allegro*, 71; *Od. Nat.* 85. 'A lawn is a plaine among trees' (Camden). Cf. L. *saltus*. The restriction of meaning to grass kept smooth in a garden is comparatively modern (Wordsworth, *White Doe of Rylstone*, canto iv. 45; Tennyson, *In Mem.* 94, &c.). The word is variously written *lawnd*, *laund*, *lande* in *Piers Plowman*, Chaucer, Surrey, Shakspere, &c.; it is the Old Fr. *lande*, Sp. *landa*, Welsh *llan*, which comes from the older Celtic *lan*, 'a place,' and originally meant an area or open space, hence a churchyard and a church, as in *Llandudno*, &c.

26] Milton's habit of early rising is illustrated in the *Apology for Smectymnuus* (quoted by Warton), where he describes himself as 'upstirring in winter often before the sound of any bell awakens men to labour or devotion; in summer as oft as the bird that first rouses, or not much tardier.' Cf. *L'Allegro*, 41 foll.; *P. L.* v. 1–25; ix. 192–200.

opening] altered from 'glimmering' in ed. 1638, from the MS. first draft; the improvement is obvious. The phrase is partly imitated by M. Bruce in his *Daphnis*, when he speaks of 'the closing lids of light.' Cf. Crashaw, *Music's Duel*, 'the eyelids of the blushing day.' Warton cites Job iii. 9 (margin); xli. 18; Soph. *Antig.* 103, ἁμέρας βλέφαρον; Middleton, *Game of Chesse* (1625), 'the opening eyelids of the morn.'

27 **drove**] probably means 'drove our flocks,' like 'drive the team afield' in Gray's *Elegy*; but the word is often used intransitively (like ἄγειν, *agere*), as in Gay's 3rd Pastoral (*Shepherd's Week*), 'Now the sun *drove* adown the western road.' The *a* in 'afield' is a dialectic form *an* of the preposition *on* (Wyatt, *Abused Lover*, 'now off, now *an*'), of which the *n* was naturally dropped before a consonant; before *h* it was sometimes omitted ('ahead,' &c.), sometimes retained

LYCIDAS.

What time the gray-fly winds her sultry horn,
Battening our flocks with the fresh dews of night,
Oft till the star that rose at evening bright   30
Toward heaven's descent had sloped his westering wheel.

('an hunting,' &c.). 'Fell on sleep' occurs in Acts xiii. 36; in Cranmer's Bible the reading was 'a building' in John ii. 20, but it is now 'in building.'

heard what time, &c.] a condensed expression for 'heard the horn of the gray-fly at the time when she sounds it.' Comp. ἀκούειν ὅτε, *audire quum*.

28] 'The gray-fly or trumpet-fly' (Warton). This cannot be the cockchaffer, as some assert, since that insect flies only in the evening. Scott, *Critical Essays*, observes that the three parts of the day, morning, noon, and evening, are clearly intended. A writer in the *Edinburgh Review* (July 1868) suggests that the 'gray-fly' may be the grig or cricket, O. E. *græg-hama*, i. e. 'gray-coat,' from its colour. For 'horn' cf. Collins, *Ode to Evening*, 'where the beetle *winds* his small but sullen *horn*.'

sultry horn] according to the classical usage by which an epithet is employed for an adverbial phrase denoting time. Farrar, *Greek Syntax*, p. 81, instances σκοταῖος ἦλθεν, 'Æneas se *matutinus* agebat,' comparing them with Dryden's 'gently they laid them down as *evening sheep*.'

29 battening] usually intransitive, 'to grow fat,' as in Shaksp. *Hamlet*, iii. 4, 'batten on this moor.' It is used transitively in J. Philips' *Cider*, bk. i., 'the meadows here with battening ooze enriched,' and in Brown's *Brit. Pastorals*, bk. ii. 1st song, 'the batning earth.' The original root is *bat-*, whence also *bet-ter* and O. E. *bét-an* (see on *l*. 64). There was an older form, *battel* (cf. Holland's *Plutarch*, 'battell soil'), whence the college term 'battels.' *Batful* = 'rich' occurs often in the *Polyolbion*.

fresh dews, &c.] Cf. Virg. *G*. iii. 324–326; *Ecl*. viii. 15.

30] See Various Readings. Keightley remarks that the evening star '*appears*, not *rises*, and it is never anywhere but *on* "heaven's descent,"' and he endeavours to save Milton from the charge of astronomical inaccuracy by interpreting the allusion of *any* star that rose about sunset. But the passage from the *Faery Queene*, III. iv. 51 ('the golden *Hesperus* was mounted high in top of heaven sheen'), which Keightley himself quotes in his note on *Comus*, *l*. 93, shows that another poet was in fact guilty of the same error. Probably both remembered the αὔλιος ἀστήρ of Apollonius (*Argonautica*, iv. 1630), which is the same as Hesperus; and it is no necessary imputation of ignorance against Milton to suppose that he meant this star both here and in the *Comus*, since he was far more likely to have erred in company with the ancients than to have corrected their mistakes by the light of modern discovery (see on *l*. 168). The amended line, inferior perhaps to the original on account of its diffuseness, is just such an expansion as a poet might easily produce, if he wished to lengthen the verse without recasting the whole passage.

31 westering] originally 'burnisht,' which, as Todd observes, is a common epithet of the sun in older poetry. Milton, however, has not so applied it elsewhere.

Meanwhile the rural ditties were not mute,
Tempered to the oaten flute ;

Between 1638 and 1645 he may have recollected Chaucer's line in *Troilus and Cresseyde*, 'the sonne gan *westrin* fast,' &c. A correspondent in *Notes and Queries* (Feb. 1873) quotes from Whittier, 'the glow of autumn's *westering* day.' 'Wested' occurs in Spenser's Introduction to the *Faery Queene*, *l.* 8, 'westing' in Cook's *Voyages*. Cf. Dryden, *Virg. G.* iv. 577, 'the *southing* sun.' The northern English form '*westling*' is used by Allan Ramsay, *Gentle Shepherd*, ii. 4, and often by Burns.

32] Imitated by R. West, *Death of Q. Caroline*—

'Meantime thy rural ditty was not mute,
Sweet bard of Merlin's cave.'

'Ditty' (*dictum*, Fr. *dicté*) means properly the words of a song as distinguished from the tune. Cf. Shaksp.*As You Like It*,v. 3, 'Though there was no great matter in the *ditty*, yet the note was very untuneable.' Hence it was applied to a short pithy poem, generally on love and its sorrows. Milton has 'amorous ditties,' *P. L.* i. 449; xi. 584. Cf. *Comus*, 86.

33 **tempered**] = 'attuned,' *P. L.* vii. 598. Warton compares Fletcher, *Purple Island*, ix. 20, 'tempering their sweetest notes unto thy lay,' and Spenser, *Ecl.* vi. 7. Gray, *Progress of Poesy*, has—

'Thee the voice, the dance obey,
Tempered to thy warbled lay.'

Cf. Petrarch, *Sonnet* xxxviii. 2, '*Temprar* potess' io in si soavi note I miei sospiri.' The Latin *temperare* is similarly used, Hor. *Od.* IV. iii. 18. Milton employs the word 'temper' in several senses, e.g. of sword metal, *P. L.* ii. 813; vi.

322; of mental constitution, *P. R.* iii. 27; of climate, *P. L.* xii. 636 (cf. Chaucer, *Assembly of Fowles*, stanza 30, 'the aire . . . so *attempre* was'); of mixing in proportion (cf. Ezek. xlvi. 14; Exod. xxix. 2). All these come from the general notion of *dividing* (perhaps in τέμ-ν-ω, *tem*-p-us, &c.), the prevailing idea being that of regular distribution and order.

oaten flute] Cf. *l.* 88 ; *Comus*, 345 ; Spenser, *Ecl.* i. 72; x. 8 &c., &c.; Collins, *Ode to Evening*, *l.* 1. 'Pipes of corn' are mentioned in Shaksp. *M. N. Dr.* ii. 2 ; Spenser, *Ecl.* ii. 40. Although the oaten pipe has been chosen by English poets as the representative of pastoral music, the classical authority for such usage is more than doubtful. Theocritus speaks only of reeds (κάλαμος, αὐλὸς, δῶναξ), 'or of the Pan's pipe (σῦριγξ). Lucretius in the celebrated passage, v. 1382 foll., adds the hemlock pipe (*cicuta*) to the *calamus* and *tibia*. Perhaps the earliest instance of *avena* in this sense is in Virg. *Ecl.* i. 2 (cf. Ov. *Met.* viii. 191 ; Tibull. III. iv. 71) ; but it is a question whether the word may not there mean any reed or hollow stalk ; Pliny, *N. H.* xix. 1, uses it of the flax-plant, 'tam gracili *avena*.' No argument can of course be drawn from the *stipula* of Virg. *Ecl.* iii. 27, where the designation is purposely disparaging. So in an Elegy to Dr. Donne by R. B.—

'all indeed
Compared to him, piped on an oaten reed ;'

and in Tickell's mock-heroic poem, *Kensington Gardens*, 'the shrill corn-pipes' are a substitute for martial trumpets in a battle of fairies.

56   LYCIDAS.

Rough Satyrs danced, and Fauns with cloven heel
From the glad sound would not be absent long,   35
And old Damœtas loved to hear our song.
  But oh ! the heavy change, now thou art gone,
Now thou art gone, and never must return !
Thee, Shepherd, thee the woods and desert caves,
With wild thyme and the gadding vine o'ergrown,   40

In this country the oaten pipe seems to have been common among rustics, and may still be met with. Burns, in a letter to Mr. Thompson (No. lxiv.), speaks of 'an oaten reed cut and notched *like that you see every shepherd boy have*,' but the sound is described as 'abominable.' Probably, therefore, our older poets took the expression from an over-literal rendering of *avena* in passages where it ought to have been understood in a wider sense.

34] Cf. Virg. *Ecl.* vi. 27, 'Tum vero in numerum Faunosque ferasque videres Ludere;' Pope, *Pastorals*, ii. 50. Newton comp. also Spenser, *Past. Ægl.* 116—

'Ye Sylvans, Fawns, and Satyrs that emong
  These thickets oft have daunced after his pipe.'[1]

If Damœtas is Mr. Chappell, the Satyrs and Fauns may represent the wilder and less studious undergraduates of Christ's. We know from a letter to Gill, 1628, that Milton had to complain of uncongenial companions at Cambridge (' cum nullos fere studiorum consortes hic reperiam, &c.'), and he may have intended to pay them a passing compliment.

36 **Old Damœtas**] is a character in Sidney's *Arcadia*, the master of the young shepherd Dorus, and described as a 'suspicious uncouth, arrant, doltish clown.' If Milton had this Damœtas in mind, the allusion to Chappell under that name may possibly show that he had not quite forgotten the old disagreement with his tutor which led to his temporary 'rustication' in 1626 (see *Eleg.* i. 11–20, Masson's *Life*, vol. i. p. 141).

37–49] Scott in his *Critical Essays* remarks that there is 'a peculiar languid melody in these lines,' and that Milton has here used 'the poetical licence by which sense is attributed to inanimate existence to great advantage.' Cf. Virg. *Ecl.* x. 13, v. 62, for the sympathy of natural objects with human sorrow and joy.

38 **never must**] = art destined never to return. Cf. *Od. Nat.* 151, 'This *must* not yet be so.'

39] Dunster cites Ovid, *Met.* xi. 43, where the beasts, woods, and rocks are said to mourn for Orpheus. For the structure of the line cf. Virg. *G.* iv. 465, ' *Te*, dulcis conjunx, *te* solo in litore secum, &c.;' Spenser, *F. Q.* IV. x. 44, ' *Thee*, goddesse, *thee* the winds, the clouds doe feare.'

40 **wild thyme**] not mentioned elsewhere by Milton. Prof. Morley quotes this line in defence of the expression 'thymy wood' in the *Epitaph*, against the objection raised that thyme does not grow in a wood. He adds a reference to Hor. *Od.* 1. xvii. 5, and to Shaksp. *M. N.*

---

[1] Faunus was represented with goat's feet, 'semicaper,' Ovid, *Fast.* v. 101.

LYCIDAS. 57

And all their echoes mourn.
The willows, and the hazel-copses green,
Shall now no more be seen
Fanning their joyous leaves to thy soft lays.
As killing as the canker to the rose, 45
Or taint-worm to the weanling herds that graze,

Dream, ii. 2, where the scene is laid in a forest.

Gadding] here simply describes the straggling nature of the vine (Cic. *de Senect.*, 'multiplici lapsu et *erratico*'), without any allusion to her desertion of the marital elm, as Warburton suggests (Hor. *Od.* IV. v. 30; *Epod.* ii. 10; Catullus, lxii. 49). *Gad*, from sb. *gad*, 'a goad' (cf. '*gad*-fly'), Icel. *gaddr*, meant 'to drive about,' and was once common. Warton quotes from a Norfolk Register of 1534 'the *Gadynge* with S. Marye Songe,' i.e. the going about with a carol to the Virgin. *Gadlyng* = 'vagrant' in Chaucer, Wyatt, &c. Cf. P. Fletcher, *Pisc. Ecl.* i. 21, 'the gadding winde;' Bacon, *Essays*, 'Envy is a gadding poison.' The word is however specially used of wives roving from home, as in *Ecclus.* xxv. 25; xxvi. 8, &c. A poet of the sixteenth century (probably John Heywood) speaks thus in praise of his lady—

'At Bacchus' feast none her shall meet,
Ne at no wanton play;
Nor gazing in the open street,
Nor *gadding* as astray.'

41] Cf. Moschus, *Epit. Bion.* 30, 'Ἀχὼ δ' ἐν πέτρῃσιν ὀδύρεται ὅττι σιωπῇ, Shelley, *Adonais*, st. xv.—

'Lost Echo sits among the voiceless mountains,
And feeds her grief with thy remembered lay.'

44 **fanning**] i.e. 'moving like a fan,' as in *P. L.* iv. 156, 'gentle gales, fanning their odoriferous wings.' Spenser, *F. Q.* I. i. 17, has, 'threatening her angry sting,' i.e. moving in a threatening manner.

45 **canker**] a crab-like tumour ('cancra') in the rose, caused by a caterpillar feeding on the blossom. Here it is used for the insect itself. Cf. Joel, i. 4, ii. 25; 2 Tim. ii. 17; James v. 3. Warton gives several references from Shakspere—e.g. *Two Gent. of Verona*, i. 1, 'In the sweetest bud the eating canker dwells;' *K. John*, iii. 4; *M. N. Dr.* ii. 3, &c. &c. It is the same word as *cancer*.

46] Sir T. Browne, *Vulgar Errors*, says: 'There is found in the summer a spider called *taint*, of a red colour.... This is accounted a deadly poison unto cows and horses. It is most unlikely that Milton should have called this insect a 'worm.' He probably refers either to the maggots or 'flukes' which infest the livers of sheep, or to the parasitic worm (*Strongylus micrurus*) which, finding its way into the bronchial tubes of young lambs, is a frequent source of disease.

weanling] a diminutive of *weanel*, from *wean*. In Spenser, *Ecl.* ix., 'a weanell waste' = a weaned lamb; Beattie translates *depulsos a lacte* (Virg. *Ecl.* vii. 15) 'my weanling lambs.' This must not be confounded with 'eanling' (*Merch. of Ven.* i. 3), which means 'just dropt,' from *ean* or *yean* (O. E. *edcnian*, 'to conceive in the womb'). 'Wean'

Or frost to flowers that their gay wardrobe wear
When first the white-thorn blows;
Such, Lycidas, thy loss to shepherd's ear.
   Where were ye, Nymphs, when the remorseless deep   50
Closed o'er the head of your loved Lycidas?
For neither were ye playing on the steep,
Where your old bards, the famous Druids, lie,

is O. E. *wenian*, G. *ge-wohnen*, to *accustom* to do without the breast.

47] Scott thinks 'simplicity is violated by making flowers wear their wardrobe.' It is difficult to see the point of this criticism. For the original reading 'buttons,' cf. Shaksp. *Hamlet*, i. 3; Browne, *Brit. Past.* ii. 3, 'Flora's choice buttons of a russet dye.' Hence the name of the flower called 'bachelor's buttons.'

50–55] This form of appeal to the Nymphs, complaining of their absence from the scene of their votary's distress, has been a favourite one with poets ever since Virgil (*Ecl.* x. 9) copied it from Theocritus (i. 66). Milton has here borrowed something from both; from the latter in making the locality of the Nymphs suit that of the catastrophe (whereas Virgil speaks of their usual haunts, Parnassus, Pindus, and Aganippe), and from the former in identifying the Nymphs with the Muses, whose favourites both Gallus and Lycidas are imagined to be. Keightley refers to Aristoph. *Nub.* 269 foll., as the original source of the idea, but the resemblance is hardly close enough to warrant the supposition that Theocritus was thinking of that passage, the circumstances and leading sentiment being quite different. The form of address (εἴτε—εἴτε, &c.) might better be compared with that in *ll.* 156 foll. of the present poem. The lines which Warton quotes from Spenser's *Astrophel*, 127 foll., are not much more than an echo of the Greek and Latin originals, since the remonstrance is there addressed, not to the Nymphs, but to shepherds and shepherdesses, who were the actual companions of Astrophel; the office of stanching the wound being in fact performed by some strange shepherds, but too late to save his life. Lord Lyttelton on the *Death of his Wife* imitates more closely:—

'Where were ye, Muses, when relentless Fate
From these fond arms your fair disciple tore?
Nor then did Pindus and Castalia's stream,
Or Aganippe's fount your steps detain, . . .
Nor where Clitumnus rolls his gentle stream.'

Cf. Shelley, *Adonais*,—

'where was lorn Urania,
   When Adonais died?'

Ossian, *Dar-thula*, 'Where have ye been, ye southern winds, when the sons of my love were deceived?'

52] 'The steep,' according to Richardson, is the hill *Ceryg y Druidion* in Denbighshire, the reputed sepulchre of the Druids. Keightley suggests the Penmaenmawr (between Conway and Bangor), but the mention of the Druids, in the absence of any special legend connecting them with that locality,

Nor on the shaggy top of Mona high,
Nor yet where Deva spreads her wizard stream.
Ay me, I fondly dream!
Had ye been there—for what could that have done?

seems to favour the former supposition.

54 shaggy top] Cf. *P. L.* vi. 645; *Comus*, 429. Drayton, *Polyolbion*, 12th Song, speaks of 'shaggy heaths.' This description of Anglesey was true only of the olden time; it was then called 'the Dark,' as Drayton tells us in the 9th Song of his *Polyolbion*, where Mona is made to say—'my brooks ... Of their huge oaks bereft to heaven so open lie, That now there's not a root discerned by any eye.' We do not know whether Milton had any personal acquaintance with these parts; Masson thinks he may possibly have visited his friend Diodati's residence on the Dee (*Eleg.* i. 3).

55] Cf. *Vac. Ex.* '98; Spenser, *F. Q.* IV. xi. 30; and the Ἀκίδος ἱερὸν ὕδωρ of Theocr. i. 69. Drayton calls the Dee the 'ominous' and the 'hallowed' flood in *Polyolb.* 10th Song; this superstition was based on the fact of its being the boundary between England and Wales, whence—

'the changing of his fords
The future ill or good of either
country told.'

In the 11th Song the epithet 'wisard' is applied to the Weever, of which it is said that—

'oft twixt him and Dee
Much strife arose in their prophetick
skill.'

Hence probably arose the notion, mentioned by Camden, that the word meant 'God's water,' and the Roman name *Deva* may have been partly owing to a similar association of ideas. Col. Robertson, *Topography of Scotland*, p. 141, derives it from the Gaelic *da-abh* (*dāv*) = 'double water' or confluence, and this is further confirmed by its Welsh name *Dyfr-dwy*, signifying the same thing.

56 Ay me] = 'Ah me,' as in *l.* 154; *P. L.* iv. 86, &c. It is probably the Spanish *Ay de mi*, and is to be distinguished from the affirmative *Ay* (G. *ja*). A correspondent of *Notes and Queries* observes that 'oh ja' is used in Southern Germany as an expression of woe—rather a curious coincidence. The Italians also say *Ahimè*.

fondly] = *foolishly*, from the p. p. of the old verb *fonne*, 'to make foolish.' The modern sense of 'indulgent' obviously arose from the idea of excessive love blinding the eyes of reason. For the primary use cf. *P. L.* iii. 470; xi. 59; Shaksp. *Coriolanus*, iv. 1, '"Tis fond to wail;' Spenser, *F. Q.* III. viii. 25, 'rudenes fond.'

57] These words will hardly bear Newton's proposed construction—'I dream *of* your having been there.' Warton would supply the ellipse after 'there'—'but why should I suppose it, for what, &c.;' a construction resembling the Greek ἀλλὰ γὰρ (ἀλλ' οὐ γὰρ οἶδα, &c.), but hardly admissible in English. A simpler way would be to refer the 'for,' &c., to the words 'I fondly dream,' i.e. 'I fondly dream *when I say* Had ye been there, &c.;' the question in *l.* 50 being of course equivalent to a wish that the Muses had been present.

What could the Muse herself that Orpheus bore,
The Muse herself for her enchanting son,
Whom universal Nature did lament,   60
When, by the rout that made the hideous roar,
His gory visage down the stream was sent,
Down the swift Hebrus to the Lesbian shore!

58–63] A comparison with the various readings of the original MS. will show that this passage is the result of most careful revision. Having first substituted the more poetical description of Calliope as 'the Muse that Orpheus bore' for the direct designation of her by name, and having got rid of the somewhat prosaic parenthesis, 'the gods farsighted bee,' Milton first introduced in the margin the words 'and heaven and hel deplore;' but afterwards erased them. 'Divine head' (of the margin) was then changed to 'goary visage,' suggested by the 'goarie scalp' of the first draft, and a final line was added to close the paragraph and to complete the rime. For the sentiment compare an epitaph by Antipater Sidonius, translated by Major Macgregor from the Greek Anthology—

'No longer, Orpheus, shalt thou charmed oaks lead;
For thou art dead! and much the Muses grieved;
Calliope, thy mother, most bereaved.
Why mourn we our dead sons, since e'en their own
To save from death no power to gods is known?'

59 **enchanting son**] Cf. *P. L.* x. 353, 'his fair *enchanting* daughter.' For the story see Ov. *Met.* xi. 1–55, 61. This passage is partly repeated in *P. L.* vii. 34 foll. *Rout* = 'company' is a favourite word with Milton (*Comus*, 542; *S. A.*

443; *P. L.* i. 747, &c.). Shakspere has 'rout of rebels,' 'merry rout,' and similar expressions. Cf. Spenser, *F. Q.* VI. ix. 8, 'the shepheard swaynes sat in a rout.' This word has the same derivation as *rout* = 'defeat,' and *route* = 'path,' all of which come in different ways from the Latin *rupta*. The similarity in sense has suggested an imaginary connexion with the Welsh *rhawd*, which has both meanings. [H. Wedgwood, according to his favourite theory of derivation from the *sound* of words (see Introduction to his *Dictionary of Etymology*), refers it to the Swedish *rjota*, 'to bellow,' comparing the O. E. *hrutan*, 'to snore;' a suggestion which the critical reader may examine for himself.]

63] Milton has been blamed for following the reading 'volucrem Hebrum' in Virg. *Æn.* i. 317, which was altered to 'Eurum' on the strength of Servius' remark, 'nam quietissimus est (Hebrus).' But Wagner and Forbiger defend the MS. reading, and compare Sil. Ital. ii. 73, 'cursuque fatigant Hebrum.' Conington observes that the same unnecessary alteration of 'Hebro' into 'Euro' was attempted in Hor. *Od.* I. xxv. 20. The rapidity of this particular river has little to do with the matter; swiftness was a general attribute of rivers, and therefore became a commonplace poetical epithet of them. Thus in Virg. *Æn.* iii. 76 Myconus

LYCIDAS.

Alas! what boots it with incessant care
To tend the homely, slighted shepherd's trade,   65
And strictly meditate the thankless Muse?
Were it not better done, as others use,

is called 'celsa,' but 'humilis' in Ov. *Met.* vii. 463, and the low-lying Prochyta is designated 'alta,' *Æn.* ix. 715, because this was a general epithet of islands. Todd comp. Davison, *Poetical Rapsodie*, 'Swift-flowing Hebrus staid all his streames in a wonder;' and Mr. Darby, in a letter to Warton (1785), quotes a statement of the Jesuit Catrou that the Hebrus is 'un fleuve d'une grande rapidité,' in direct contradiction to the assertion of Servius.

the Lesbian shore] Ov. *Met.* xi. 55, *l.c.*, 'Methymnæi potiuntur litore Lesbi.' According to common tradition the head of Orpheus was carried by the waves to Lesbos, and there buried, for which pious office the Lesbians were rewarded with the gift of preeminence in song.

64–84] The pastoral landscape now disappears, and the shepherd merges into the poet (see *Introduction*). 'What use is there in all this laborious pursuit of learning, when life is so uncertain?' Phœbus interposes with 'a strain of higher mood,' reminding the questioner that fame, which is the reward of noble deeds, lives on after death in heaven. The rural muse, though momentarily recalled at *l.* 85, does not permanently reappear till *l.* 132.

what boots it] Cf. *Richard II.* i. 3; *Winter's Tale*, iii. 2, &c. 'Boot' is O. E. *bôt*, whence *bêtan*, 'to improve,' from same root as *batten* (*l.* 29).

incessant] in ed. 1638 'uncessant.' The two forms seem to have been used indiscriminately about this period; we find 'unexpressive,'

l. 176, *Od. Nat.* 116; 'ingrateful,' *P. L.* v. 407; 'increate,' *ib.* iii. 6. Shakspere has 'unpossible,' 'uneffectual,' 'unperfect' (see Bible version of Ps. cxxxix. 16) along with 'ingrateful,' 'infortunate,' &c.

65] Cf. Spenser, *Ecl.* vi. 67, 'homely shepherd's quill.'

66 meditate the Muse] a literal translation of Virgil, *Ecl.* i. 2, 'Musam meditaris' (μελετᾶν). This is one instance among many of Milton's habit of verbally adopting classical phrases (cf. 11, 20 *supra*). Perhaps the most remarkable cases are the 'thick drop serene' (*P. L.* iii. 25), from *gutta serena*, and the 'happy-making sight' (*Ode on Time*, 18), from *Visio Beatifica*. Virgil meant simply 'compose a *song*,' a meaning which 'Muse' will not bear in English, although it cannot go with 'meditate' in any other sense. It is therefore doubtful whether Milton intended 'thankless' to be intransitive, i.e. 'the poetry which gets no thanks,' or transitive, i.e. 'the Muse who though courted with pains yet proves ungrateful.' For the former sense cf. Surrey, *Transl. of Virg. Æn.* ii. 113, 'these thankless tales,' and the two meanings of *ingratus*, 'ungrateful' and 'unrequited.'

67] The reading of 1638, 'do' for 'use,' is an error of the press, caused by the word 'done,' preceding.

as others use] alluding to the fashionable erotic poetry of the day (as represented by Herrick, Wither, Lovelace, &c., *l.* 69 *note*), with which Milton's severer taste did not accord. From his 7th Elegy, however, we learn that he had once yielded to a

.To sport with Amaryllis in the shade,
Or with the tangles of Neæra's hair!
Fame is the spur that the clear spirit doth raise—   70
That last infirmity of noble mind—

softer passion, which the more serious pursuits of college life soon dispelled—
'Donec Socraticos umbrosa Academia rivos
  Præbuit, admissum dedocuitque jugum.'
It has been plausibly argued that there is in the next two lines a special reference to two Latin poems by G. Buchanan (who was one of Milton's favourite authors), addressed to Amaryllis and Neæra respectively. As regards the latter, the allusion seems highly probable; since the poet distinctly describes himself as a prisoner bound by Cupid with a lock of Neæra's hair—
'Deinde unum evellens ex auricomante capillum
  Vertice captivis vincla dedit manibus.'
It is true that the Amaryllis of Buchanan represents the city of Paris, and not an actual lady; but Milton may easily have overlooked or ignored this fact. The probability of the reference is strengthened by the first MS. reading, '*Hid in* the tangles, &c.;' since our poet would hardly have committed the absurdity of representing a lover sporting with one mistress, and at the same time being entangled in the hair of another, unless some such literary association had confused the two names in his mind. The present passage is imitated by Soame Jenyns in his *Immortality of the Soul*—
'Were it not wiser far, supinely laid,
To sport with Phyllis in the noontide shade?'

68] Amaryllis and Neæra are two of the common representative names in ancient pastoral song. Cf. Virg. *Ecl.* i. 31; ii. 14; iii. 3, 81; ix. 22. Ἀμάρυλλις (ἀμαρύσσω), the 'sparkling beauty,' is the subject of Theocritus' 3rd Idyll. Both names occur together in Ariosto, *Orl. Fur.* xi. 12.

69] Cf. Lovelace, *To Althea*, 'When I lie tangled in her hair.'

70] This sentiment is common in the classics. Newton instances Cic. *Pro Archia*, c. 10, 'trahimur omnes laudis studio, et optimus quisque maxime gloria ducitur.' Cf. Spenser, *Tears of the Muses*, 454, 'due praise that is the spur of doing well.' It is vividly illustrated in the *Faery Queene*, II. vii. 46 foll., where Philotime is described as holding a golden chain reaching to heaven, 'every linck whereof was a step of dignity,' and by which the crowd were striving 'to climb aloft.' It reappears in the *Paradise Regained*, iii. 24 foll., in an enlarged form from the mouth of Satan tempting our Lord to ambition, where the phrase 'erected spirits' (*l.* 27) may perhaps explain the '*clear* spirit' of this passage, i.e. purified by elevation into a *clearer* atmosphere. Keightley takes it to mean 'illustrious,' It. *chiaro*. The identical expression 'clear spirit' is cited by Todd from Milton's *Prose Works*, vol. i. p. 161.
Scott (*Critical Essays*) doubts the correctness of representing Fame 'both as a motive and as a reward.' But surely the desire of Fame acts as a motive during the toil of action, and when realised in attainment becomes its final reward.

71] Athenæus in his *Deipnosophistæ* (xi. 15, § 116) represents Plato

To scorn delights, and live laborious days;
But the fair guerdon when we hope to find,
And think to burst out into sudden blaze,
Comes the blind Fury with the abhorred shears, 75
And slits the thin-spun life. 'But not the praise,'
Phœbus replied, and touched my trembling ears,
'Fame is no plant that grows on mortal soil,

as saying ἔσχατον τὸν τῆς δόξης χιτῶνα ἐν τῷ θανάτῳ αὐτῷ ἀποδυόμεθα. Cf. Tacitus, *Hist.* iv. 6, 'etiam sapientibus cupido gloriæ novissima exuitur,' of which the line quoted by Warton from Massinger's *Very Woman*, 'though the desire of fame be the last weakness wise men put off,' is nearly a literal translation. Of pride Bp. Hall says, 'Pride is the inmost coat, which we put on first and put off last.'

73 guerdon] This word is not elsewhere found in Milton's poems, but is common in Spenser (*F. Q.* I. vii. 15; II. vi. 28, &c.). Though it occurs at least as early as Chaucer, it seems to have become obsolete in the sixteenth century, being explained in the Glossary to the *Shepheard's Kalendar* (see on *l.* 2); and even as late as 1730 it was thought to require a note in a poem by West on *Education*. Most readers will remember the scene in *Love's Labour's Lost*, iii. 1, where Costard the clown exclaims, 'O sweet *guerdon*, better than *remuneration*,' taking each word to mean a sum of money. (For the derivation see Appendix I.).

74] Cf. *P. R.* iii. 47, *l. c.*; Chapman's *Homer's Il.* xvii. 177, 'that frail *blaze* of excellence that neighbours death.' Pindar (*Nem.* x. 4) uses φλέγεσθαι in the same sense.

75 blind Fury] Cf. Spenser, *Ruines of Rome*, st. 24. Milton here purposely in indignation calls Atropos a Fury, and not without

classical authority; for in an Orphic Hymn (quoted by Sympson) the θεαὶ μοῖραι are styled ὀφιοπλόκαμοι, which is a proper epithet of the Furies. Langhorne in his *Elegy on the Death of Handel* speaks of 'the grim fury's breast.' Cf. Lloyd, *Tears and Triumph of Parnassus*—

'Where were ye Muses (*l.* 50 *supra*) when the fatal shears
The Fury raised to close his reverend years?'

For the 'shears of destiny' see Shaksp. *K. John*, v. 2.

76] According to the old verse—
'Clotho colum retinet, Lachesis net, et *Atropos occat.*'

For 'slit' in the sense of cutting across, instead of lengthwise, Keightley cites Golding's *Ovid. Met.* xii. 248—

'Like one that with an ax doth *slit* An ox's neck in sacrifice.'

But not the praise] i.e. 'the praise is not intercepted' (Warton). This is a kind of *zeugma*, the verb 'slits' being strictly applicable to the thread alone, but suggesting another verb of similar meaning to govern 'praise.'

77] From Virg. *Ecl.* vi. 3, where Conington remarks that touching the ear was a symbolical act, the ear being the seat of memory.

78] Cf. Pindar, *Nem.* vii. 45, τιμὰ δὲ γίγνεται, &c., i.e. 'true honour is theirs whose glorious fame

Nor in the glistering foil
Set off to the world, nor in broad rumour lies,   80
But lives and spreads aloft by those pure eyes

the god exalteth, an aid to their memory after death' (τεθνακότων βοαθόον).

79, 80] Thus translated by Plumptre (1797)—

οὐδ' ἐνὶ κιβδήλοις ἀρετᾶν ζαλώμασι κεῖται
ἄντινα τῶν πολλῶν θάμβει καὶ ἀγάζεται ὄχλος.

And by Mathias (see note on *l.* 19)—

'Non mai d' orpel fallace
Con mentito splendor sfavilla al mondo,
Dello spanto romor nemica, Fama.'

Milton's words admit of a twofold construction. The first is—' Nor is it (Fame) set off to the world in (i.e. *by*) the glistering foil, nor does it lie (consist) in a wide reputation.' In this case 'foil' must be understood in a sense which it often bears elsewhere, of a dark substance (originally a thin *leaf* of metal), in which jewels were placed to 'set off' their lustre. Cf. Shaksp. *Rich. II.* i. 3—

'a *foil* wherein thou art to set
The precious jewel of thy home return;'

1 *Hen. IV.* i. 2 (quoted by Warton), ' And like bright metal on a sullen ground, &c.' In *Rich. III.* v. 3 the stone of Scone set in the oak chair of Edward I. is called

'a base foul stone,
Made precious by the *foil* of England's chair.'

Chr. Brook in an *Epithalamium* (speaking of a newly wedded bride) says—

'Then let the dark *foyle* of the geniall bed

Extend her brightness to his inward sight.'

But this mode of taking the words fails to give a suitable meaning to the passage. It is not Fame itself which is 'set off to the world,' but the life and actions of the man, the display of which before the eyes of the public constitutes fame—at least according to the vulgar notion which Milton is here combating. The true sense seems to be this: 'Nor does it (true Fame) consist in the specious appearance *which is* displayed to the world, nor in a widespread renown.' *Fame* will then be the subject of the verb *lies*, and *set off* a participle agreeing with *foil*; the preposition *in* before 'glistering foil' will have the same construction and sense as the *in* before 'broad rumour,' both phrases being constructed after *lies*. And the meaning of 'foil' will be, not exactly 'leaf-gold,' as Newton takes it (comparing the 'golden foile' of Spenser, *F. Q.* I. iv. 4), but *tinsel*, i.e. some baser metal which glitters like gold, and makes a fair show to the eye. Scott doubts 'whether the metaphor of "plant" is continued to this line or not,' and imagines 'a plant with leaves artificially gilded.' Perhaps the idea of 'foil' (*folium*) was suggested by the word 'plant,' but the metaphor itself is not resumed till *l.* 81 in the words 'lives and spreads,' which describe the growth of a tree.

81 by] probably = 'near,' i.e. 'in presence of.' Shaksp. *Twelfth Night*, iii. 1, 'Thou mayest say the king lives *by* a beggar, if a beggar dwell *near* him.' So we still say 'hard *by*.' This seems better than

l perfect witness of all-judging Jove ;
he pronounces lastly on each deed,
so much fame in Heaven expect thy meed.'
) fountain Arethuse, and thou honoured flood, 85
)oth-sliding Mincius, crowned with vocal reeds,
it strain I heard was of a higher mood.
now my oat proceeds,
l listens to the herald of the sea,

;htley's explanation, 'by means
; lastly] in the somewhat un-
l sense of 'finally' or 'decisive-
'a literal rendering of *ulti-*
x. Cf. Hor. *Od.* I. xvi. 19,
s urbibus *ultimæ* Stetere causæ,
' i.e. the final (ultimate) cause
ieir ruin.
meed] See on *l.* 14, and cf.
iser, *F. Q.* III. x. 31, 'Fame is
need and glory, virtue's pay.'
;–102] The return after the di-
sion is marked by an invocation
he pastoral fountain Arethusa,
of Virgil's native river, the
cius—a practical recognition of
Sicilian and Roman pastorals
filton's own originals (see In-
uction). For the story of Are-
a see Ovid, *Met.* v. 579 foll.
[oschus, *Epitaphium Bionis,* 83,
is said to have 'drunk of
husa's fount,' and in Theocr. *Id.*
7 the dying Daphnis exclaims,
'Ἀρέθουσα. Virgil (*Ecl.* x. 1)
kes her as a Muse inspiring
ong.
moured flood] imitated by West
is *Monody on Q. Caroline,* 'O
ured flood with reeds Pierian
ned, Isis!' Here the epithet
/en to the river because of its
:iation with Virgil.
] Cf. Sylvester, *Du Bartas,*
'the crystal of smooth-sliding
s.' This and the 'vocal reeds'
rom Virgil, *Georg.* iii. 14, 'tardis

ubi flexibus errat Mincius, et tenera
prætexit arundine ripas.' The epithet 'vocal' is best illustrated by
the passage in Lucretius, v. 1383
foll., alluded to on *l.* 33.
87] An apology to the rural muse
for departing from the pastoral
strain, under the irresistible influence of Phœbus. A similar device
is adopted after the next digression
(*l.* 132).
mood] (*P. L.* i. 550 ; *S. A.* 661)
= 'character,' from *modus,* signifying a particular arrangement of intervals in the musical scale, the
study of which formed so important
an element in the Greek system of
education (Plato, *Republic,* B. iii. ;
Aristotle, *Politics,* B. viii.). The
word has nothing to do with a
'mood' or *state of mind,* which is
O. E. *mód,* G. *muth,* 'impulse,'
though the similarity of meaning
might easily cause confusion.
88] See on *l.* 33. Here the instrument, of course, stands for the
poem. A still bolder expression
occurs in the 6th Elegy, *l.* 89, where
patriis meditata cicutis means 'composed in my native tongue.' In
Landor's *Imaginary Conversations*
(Southey and Landor) this line is
curiously misquoted, 'now my *oar*
proceeds ;' upon which Southey is
supposed to remark, 'Does the *oar*
listen?'
89 listens] i.e. like a pupil
(ἀκροατής), to learn what he is to say

LYCIDAS.

6 That came in Neptune's plea. 90
He asked the waves, and asked the felon winds,
What hard mishap hath doomed this gentle swain?
And questioned every gust of rugged wings
That blows from off each beaked promontory.
7 They knew not of his story; 95
And sage Hippotades their answer brings,

upon the subject. The 'herald' is Triton, the son of Neptune; his instrument was the *concha* or spiral shell (Virg. *Æn.* vi. 171; x. 209), and his office of herald is illustrated in Ovid, *Met.* i. 333 foll., where he is ordered to sound a retreat for the waters of the deluge ('cecinit jussos receptus').

90] Keightley understands 'Neptune's plea' to mean the judicial enquiry which Neptune deputed Triton to hold; and he instances the 'Court of Common *Pleas*,' &c., as examples of the word in this signification. But it seems better to take it in its usual sense of a statement made by the defendant to satisfy (*placere*) the court; here the excuse offered by Neptune and conveyed by Triton. Milton probably intended to represent Neptune himself as involved in the blame, and desirous to clear himself by a strict enquiry applied to his subordinates. Plumptre adopts this view when he translates Ποσειδάωνος ἀμυντήρ.

91 felon] (MS. 'fellon') = 'cruel,' if it comes from *fell*, with the additional sense of 'criminal,' the winds being introduced as culprits about to be tried. For the etymology see Appendix I.

93 wings] misprinted 'winds' in Tonson's edition of 1705, and in Newton's of 1785, probably on account of 'winds' in *l.* 91. 'Gust of wings' is the gen. of quality = 'winged gusts,' and 'rugged' = 'ragged,' i.e. broken by intervening obstacles. *Rugged* and *ragged* seem to have been used indiscriminately about this period (*L'Allegro*, 9; Isaiah ii. 21), but they are distinct words, the former being allied to the O. E. *ruh*, 'rough,' the latter to Swed. *ragg* = 'shaggy hair.'

94] Warton compares *P. L.* xi. 746; Drayton, *Polyolbion*, 1st Song, 'the utmost end of Cornwal's furrowing *beak.*' Pliny, *Nat. Hist.* A. 49, uses 'rostrum' for the promontory of an island in the Nile.

95 his story] i.e. how to give any account of him.

96] Warton observes that Hippotades is not a common name of Æolus, and does not occur in Virgil. He quotes Homer, *Od.* x. 2; Ovid, *Met.* iv. 661; xiv. 86, &c., and passages from the *Argonautica* of Apoll. Rhodius and Val. Flaccus. The epithet 'sage' implies authority and responsibility. Dunster thinks there is a special allusion to 'sciret' in Virg. *Æn.* i. 63, which is however there qualified by the addition of 'jussus' and of 'fœdere certo.' Homer, *Od.* x. 21, represents Æolus as acting by his own discretion (παυέμεναι ἠδ' ὀρνύμεν ὅν κ' ἐθέλῃσι). Richardson understands 'sage' of his foreknowledge of the weather; but this is a later and rationalised form of the story, and one which Milton as a poet is not likely to have chosen, since even when writing history he professes himself unwilling to give up the myths entirely, rejecting only those

LYCIDAS. 67

That not a blast was from his dungeon strayed;
The air was calm, and on the level brine
Sleek Panopè with all her sisters played.
It was that fatal and perfidious bark,   100
Built in the eclipse, and rigged with curses dark,
That sunk so low that sacred head of thine.
    Next Camus, reverend sire, went footing slow,
His mantle hairy and his bonnet sedge,·

which are 'impossible and absurd' *Hist. of Britain*, c. 1, and see wrote, *Hist. of Greece*, vol. i. c. 17).

98 level brine] imitated by J. Warton in his *Enthusiast* (1740), 'the dolphin dancing o'er the level brine.'

99 Panope] one of the fifty daughters of Nereus and Doris Hesiod, *Theog*. 250 foll.). The same Πανόπη, denoting a *wide view over a calm expanse of water*, is significant here, as also in Virg. *Georg*. i. 437, *Æn*. v. 240, 823. Spenser (apparently on his own authority) introduces her as an 'old nymph' who kept the house of Proteus (*F. Q.* III. viii. 37).

100] See the inscription prefixed to the *Cambridge Verses* of 1638, *navi in scopulum allisa, et rimis ictu fatiscente.*

101] Warton comp. Shaksp. *Macbeth*, iv. 1—
    'slips of yew,
Slivered (cut) in the moon's eclipse,'
used by the witches for their incantations. The superstition about eclipses as portents of impending calamity is an old one (Virg. *Georg*. . 465 foll., and cf. *P. L.* i. 597 foll.); hence might naturally arise the belief that work done during an eclipse was likely to fail of success; but there seems to be no evidence to show that the ancients actually so regarded it.

102 sacred] consecrated by friendship, and therefore inviolable. Cf. Tennyson, *In Memoriam*, xiv. 10, 'the man I held as half divine.'

103 Camus] So in Spenser's *Pastorall Æglogue* the Thames, Humber, Severn, and other rivers mourn for their favourite bard Phillisides. Cowley, *Complaint*, l. 6, speaks of 'reverend Cam.' 'Sire' is the usual mythological designation of a river, as a presiding and protecting power. Cf. Livy, ii. 10, 'Tiberine pater;' Virg. *Æn*. viii. 31. What follows is an adaptation of the natural features of the locality to the circumstances of mourning, but without the unpleasant associations which appear in the 'nuda arva' and 'juncosas Cami paludes' of the 1st Elegy, *ll*. 13, 89. That Milton had no great affection for Cambridge is clear (see on *ll*. 34, 36), but this was not a fit occasion for expressing any such feeling. With 'footing slow' Keightley compares *F. Q.* I. iii. 10, 'A damsel spied slow footing her before.' Cf. Duncombe, *Ode to C. P.*—

    'where sedgy Cam
Bathes with slow pace his academic grove.'

Those who are acquainted with the locality will recognise the appropriateness of these descriptions; it may not be out of place to mention the fact, that in a report addressed

Inwrought with figures dim, and on the edge 105
Like to that sanguine flower inscribed with woe.
'Ah! who hath reft,' quoth he, 'my dearest pledge?'
Last came, and last did go,

to the Cambridge Improvement Commissioners (Oct. 1871) by Mr. J. B. Denton, 'the sluggish nature of the river' is expressly noted as one of the main difficulties in the way of the proposed operations.

105] In the 'figures dim' Warburton sees a reference to the 'fabulous traditions of the high antiquity of Cambridge.' Perhaps we need hardly look for any such precise application of the expression, which may very well be a part of the general picture of desolation. Dunster's remark that 'on sedge-leaves, when dried, there are certain dim, indistinct, and dusky streaks on the edge,' is worth noticing, and the original reading 'scrauled ore' seems to favour the probability of such an allusion.

106] For the legend of Hyacinthus (to which Milton also alludes in the Ode on the *Death of a Fair Infant*, 25 foll.) see Ovid, *Met.* x. 210 foll. 'Ipse suos gemitus foliis inscribit et Ai Ai Flos habet inscriptum' (*ib.* 215). Hence Theocritus, x. 28, calls the flower à γραπτὰ ὑάκινθος, and Moschus, *Epit. Bion. l.* 6, exclaims νῦν ὑάκινθε λάλει τὰ σὰ γράμματα. Cf. Drummond, *Epit. on Prince Henry*—

'that sweet flower that bears
In sanguine spots the tenour of our woe.'

107 reft] (O. E. *reſian*, to rob) now commonly appears in its compound *be-reave*. The simple verb occurs nowhere else in Milton, but is frequently used by the Elizabethan poets, e.g. Shakspere, *Much Ado*, iv. 1, *All's Well*, v. 3, &c.; Surrey, *passim* ; Spenser, *F. Q.* I. iii. 36, 41, &c. Sir W. Raleigh, *Cynthia*, says of the moon, 'she that from the sun *reaves* power and might.'

pledge] = offspring, considered as a security of conjugal fidelity. *Pignus* in this sense is very common, cf. Propert. IV. xi. 73, 'communia pignora natos.' Milton has 'pignora cara,' *Eleg.* iv. 42. Warton quotes from the *Rime Spirituali* of Angelo Grillo 'mio caro *pegno*.' Cf. *P. L.* ii. 818 ; Ode *At a Solemn Musick, l.* 1; Spenser, *F. Q.* I. x. 4 ; Bacon, *Essay on Marriage*, 'their dearest pledges ;' Lord Lyttelton, on the death of Lady L.—

'Nor did she crown our mutual flame
With pledges dear, and with a father's tender name.'

108] Neve in his *Cursory Remarks on some English Poets* (1789) observes that 'as Dante has made Cato of Utica keeper of the gates of Purgatorio, Milton has here in return placed St. Peter in company with Apollo, Triton, &c.,' and that 'for the intrusion respecting the clergy of his time the earliest Italians have set plentiful example.' See for instance St. Peter's animadversions upon the degeneracy of his successors in *Paradiso*, Canto 27, which closely resembles the present passage. Dante does not however make Cato the 'keeper of the gates' (that office being given to an angel, *Purgat.* ix. 78, 105), but the guardian of certain wandering spirits outside the place itself. For the charge of irreverence urged against Milton for his alleged confusion of things sacred and profane see Introduction, p. 22.

LYCIDAS. 69

The pilot of the Galilean lake ;
Two massy keys he bore of metals twain—   110
The golden opes, the iron shuts amain.
He shook his mitred locks, and stern bespake :

109 **Pilot**] is an addition to the gospel narrative (Luke v. 3), where there is no intimation that Peter acted in that capacity towards the others. He was doubtless the *steersman* of his own ship, a sense in which 'pilot' is often used (*P. L.* i. 204; *S. A.* 198). In *l.* 1044 of the latter poem the 'pilot' and 'steersmate' are distinguished.

110] Originally from Matt. xvi. 19, where the number of keys is not mentioned. From the earliest times St. Peter was represented with *two* keys ; hence P. Fletcher in his *Locusts* (quoted by Todd) says of the Pope—

'In his hand two golden keys he beares,
To open heaven and hell and shut againe ;'

and in the *Purple Island*, vii. 421, *Dichostasis* (Schism) is invested with the same authority. Dante (*Inferno*, xxvii.) makes Pope Boniface say—

'Lo ciel poss' io serrare e disserrare,
Come tu sai ; però son due le chiavi.'

In the ode *In Quintum Novembris* Milton speaks merely of 'Apostolicæ custodia clavis.' The distinction between the two metals— one denoting the value of the benefits secured by admission, the other stern severity in exclusion—is our poet's own ; in the parallel passage of Dante, *Purg.* ix. 120 foll., both a golden and a silver key are used by the angel to *open* the gate. The Italian proverb quoted by Mr. Bowles, 'Con le chiavi d' oro s' apre ogna porta,' alludes to the influence of money, and has therefore nothing to do with the 'power of the keys.'

111 **amain**] = 'firmly,' lit. ' with might,' from O. E. *mægen*, a derivative of *magan*, 'to be strong.' For the prefix *a* see on *l.* 27.

112] It would be unfair to construe this admission of the *mitre* into a precise statement of Milton's religious views at this period, or to suppose with Warburton that 'it sharpened his satire to have the prelacy condemned by one of their own order.' As St. Peter here speaks with episcopal authority, he is made to wear the distinctive dress of his order. So in the 3rd Elegy (1626) on the Bishop of Winchester, the glorified prelate is represented with the 'infula' or mitre upon his head (*l.* 56). In the *Reason of Church Government*, c. vi. (1641) Milton indeed uses very different language, when he speaks of 'the haughty prelates with their forked mitres, the badge of schism ;' but the events of the three intervening years had produced a considerable change in his attitude towards the clergy, or at least had emboldened him in the expression of opinions, which had been long lurking in his mind, and of which the present invective is perhaps the earliest intimation.

bespake] here used absolutely, as in *P. R.* i. 43 ; *Ode Nat.* 76. Cf. Spens. *F. Q.* I. ii. 32, 'he thus bespake.' The prefix *be-* is the same as *by* (= 'near' or 'to'), with the addition of the person addressed. *P. L.* iv. 1005, 'Gabriel

How well could I have spared for thee, young swain,
Enow of such as, for their bellies' sake,
Creep, and intrude, and climb into the fold!   115
Of other care they little reckoning make,

. . thus bespake the fiend.' At the present day it usually = 'speak for,' i.e. 'secure beforehand,' and sometimes 'declare' or 'show,' as in Cowper's *Task*, ii. 702, 'His head . . bespoke him;' Poems by Jane Taylor, 'the cheerful chimes bespeak the hour of prayer.'

113-131] Three grounds of complaint are here alleged—(1) the covetousness and moral corruption of the clergy, (2) their false or imperfect doctrine, (3) another evil, distinct from the former, but not expressly defined, which is most probably to be understood of the increasing perversions to Romanism so frequent at this period. (See Appendix II.).

114 enow] printed 'anow' in ed. 1645 (in the MS. 'anough'). It is spelt both ways in the *Areopagitica* (1644). So 'emong' and 'among,' &c. In Shaksp. *Merch. of Venice*, ii. 2, we find 'aleven' for 'eleven' (see Dyce *ad loc.*).

for their bellies' sake] Cf. Ezek. xxxiv. 2, 3. On what follows Warton remarks that Milton has copied from Spenser's 5th Eclogue the sentiments of Piers the Protestant shepherd, which are quoted at full length in the *Animadversions on the Remonstrant's Defence* (1641). Our author's prose works abound with specimens of similar language; e.g. in the *Apology for Smectymnuus* he speaks of 'the prelate, who being a pluralist may under one surplice hide four benefices;' and many similar passages might be quoted. Compare also the following lines, addressed to the clergy in the tragedy of *Baptistes*, translated from the Latin of G. Buchanan in 1637,

and sometimes, but without sufficient reason, attributed to Milton—

'Then like dumb dogs that bark not here, you fret
And fume about your sheepcotes; but the wolves
Which of you drive away? The wolves, said I?
You are the wolves yourselves, that flay your flocke,
Clothed with their wool; their milk don't slack your thirst,
Their flesh your hunger. Thus yourselves you feed,
But not your flock.'

115] Cf. *P. L.* iv. 193. T. Becon, chaplain to Cranmer (about 1540), says in his *Policy of War*—'They come into their benefices *non per ostium sed aliunde*, for the desire of filthy lucre' (St. John x. 1). By intrusion into the fold Milton does not imply absence or invalidity of orders; his matured views concerning a minister's credentials were afterwards clearly set forth in the treatise on *Christian Doctrine*, c. 29, 31. These are 'spiritual knowledge and sanctity of life,' to be tested by previous trial, and the choice is to belong to the people collectively; a mode of proceeding which Hooker (*Eccl. Pol.* vii. 14) argues to be a mere pretence, since the elders 'allow not their own previous choice to be set aside by their [the people's] disapprobation;' and he ludicrously compares it to the way of 'nurses with infants, whose mouths they besmear with the backside of the spoon, as though they had fed them, when they themselves devour the food.'

116, 117] Cf. Becon, *Jewel of*

Than how to scramble at the shearers' feast,
And shove away the worthy bidden guest.
Blind mouths! that scarce themselves know how to hold
A sheep-hook, or have learned aught else the least 120

Joy—'Our spiritual men are led with no care of feeding Christ's flock... Christ's threefold *Pasce* is turned into the Jews' double *Tolle*. They feed nothing except themselves, they toll and catch whatsoever they may.'

118 **the worthy bidden guest**] Matt. xxii. 8. Milton here allows the *principle* of emolument for ministerial services, since 'the shearers' feast' is the due reward of honest shepherds; latterly his opinions on this subject were somewhat modified. In the Treatise entitled *The Likeliest Means to remove Hirelings* and in the *Christian Doctrine*, while barely admitting that 'the labourer is worthy of his hire,' he restricts it to voluntary contributions, adding that 'it is more desirable to serve gratuitously,' and to support themselves (if need be) 'by the exercise of some trade or calling' (*C. D.* c. 31).

119] The phrase 'blind mouths' may be illustrated from the classical usage of transferring to one bodily sense the functions of another; e.g. Soph. *Œd. T.* 371, τυφλὸς τὰ ὦτα, Val. Flacc. ii. 461, 'cæcus clamor,' Plin. *N. H.* xxxvii. 18, 'surdus color,' &c. The shepherds are emphatically termed 'mouths,' first for their gluttony, secondly in reference to their preaching. As regards the former cf. Hesiod, *Theog.* 26, where the Heliconian swains are said to be γαστέρες οἶον, 'nothing but bellies.' Cf. γαστέρες ἀργαί ('lazy gluttons'), St. Paul to Titus, i. 12; Pliny, *N. H.* ix. 17, 30, 'proceres gulæ' ('noble gluttons'). Hogg (1694) translates the present passage 'O *cæci ventres*, qui vix comprendere dextra Pastorale pedum, aut aliquid didicere, &c.' Next by a bold figure of speech the 'mouths' are said 'to hold a sheep-hook,' with which Newton aptly compares Hor. *Sat.* II. ii. 39—

'Porrectum magno magnum *spectare* catino
Vellem *ait* Harpyiis *gula* digna rapacibus;'

also *P. L.* v. 711, 'the eternal *eye* ...saw...and smiling *said*.' As to the relative importance of *preaching*, Milton places it foremost among ministerial duties, even above the administration of sacraments (*C. D.* c. 29). To a Puritan 'a non-preaching ministry' was a crying evil, and even James I. at the Hampton Court Conference of 1604 gives his opinion that 'a preaching ministry is best,' though he orders 'that praying be attended to as well.' At the same Conference the daily use of the Book of Homilies, originally set forth in 1562 to remedy the defects of the clergy on this head (see *Preface to Homilies*), was strictly enjoined; and some twenty years later the *King's Letters* were issued for the express purpose of restraining extravagances in the pulpit (Fuller, *Church Hist.* X. vii. 4).

120 **sheep-hook**] κορύνη, Theocr. *Id.* vii. 43; 'pedum,' Virg. *Ecl.* v. 88. Cf. Treatise on *Reformation in England*, B. ii., 'the pastorly rod and sheep-hook of Christ' (Psalm xxiii. 4). Of unlearned ministers Becon remarks in his Preface, 'They leap into the pulpits

That to the faithful herdman's art belongs!
What recks it them? What need they? They are sped;
And, when they list, their lean and flashy songs

without shame, when they understand not what pulpit matters mean. They teach before they learn.' Milton's earlier opinions were in favour of a learned clergy, as might have been expected from the circumstances of his education. In a letter to the elder Gill from Cambridge, 1628, he deplores the ignorance of those 'who without any acquaintance with criticism or philosophy engage in the study of theology' (*Epist. Fam.* 3). But in the *Likeliest Way &c.* (1651) he contemptuously designates all such learning as 'scholastical trash,' adding that every requisite 'may be easily attained, and by the meanest capacities, if they seek the guidance of the Holy Spirit,' an opinion which is further developed in the *Christian Doctrine*, c. 31.

121 **herdman's**] ('heard.rmans' in the MS.), here = 'shepherd's.' The original meaning is simply 'one who tends or watches' (G. *Herde, hirten*, &c.) either sheep or larger cattle, and the modern distinction was not always observed. Spenser, *F. Q.* VI. xi. 37, 39, uses 'heards' and 'heardgroomes' for keeper of sheep, though he elsewhere (*ib.* ix. 10) makes a difference—'ne was there *heard*, ne was there *shepheard's* swayne.' In the Bible the spelling is always 'herdman' (Gen. xiii. 7; xxvi. 20; Amos i. 1; vii. 14, &c.).

122 **recks it them**] (O. E. *rec*, 'care.') Cf. *Comus*, 401; Gower, *Confessio Amantis*, B. v., 'him recketh not.' The verb is generally personal, as in *P. L.* ii. 50; ix. 173; Spens. *Ecl.* vii. 34, 'thou *rekes* much of thy swincke (toil).'

they are sped] i.e. 'are provided for' (Keightley). So in the *Merchant of Venice*, ii. 9, the Prince of Arragon, reading his fortune on the scroll in the silver casket, finds the words 'Begone, you are *sped*.' In Judges v. 30 the mother of Sisera, awaiting the return of her son whom she supposed victorious, exclaims 'Have they not *sped?*' The same sense of the word lingers in the expression 'God speed you.' Of the luxurious habits of prelates Milton speaks in the *Apology for Smectymnuus*, 'They let hundreds of families famish in one diocese, while they themselves enjoy that wealth that would furnish all those dark places with ample supply.'

123 **when they list**] i.e. even this miserable pittance is doled out to the flock only at such time as is convenient to the shepherds. That the 'lean and flashy songs' represent unsound oral instruction is plain from the context; but in the pastoral prototype singing and piping are the *recreation*, not the business of shepherds, and the meaning ought simply to be that the spiritual pastors amuse themselves instead of tending their flocks. In that case however there would be no point in the allusion to the wretched quality of the music, which could in no way affect the welfare of the sheep. The confusion of metaphor thus involved needs simply stating to be apparent; the true analogy lies in the unhealthiness of pasture, to which a sudden transition is made in *l.* 126.

flashy] Todd quotes from Milton's *Colasterion*, in which he calls his opponent's arguments 'the *flashiest*, the fustiest that ever corrupted such an unswilled hogshead.' Dry-

Grate on their scrannel pipes of wretched straw;
The hungry sheep look up, and are not fed,   125
But, swollen with wind and the rank mist they draw,

den, *Transl. of Persius*, Sat. i., has
'flashy wit,' and Bacon, *Essay on Studies*, says 'distilled books are flashy things.'

124] Imitated from Virg. *Ecl.* iii. 26, 'stridenti miserum stipula disperdere carmen.' Plumptre translates (keeping the alliteration)—

οἱ καλαμαῖς, εὖτ' ἂν γ' ἐθέλοντι, πονηραῖς
κοῦφα μέλη τρίσδοντες ἄσαρκ' ἀπόμουσα κρέκοντι.

The word 'scrannel' does not seem to have been used by any *previous* writer; Newton does not remember to have seen it elsewhere at all. He might however have found it in Langhorne's *Fables of Flora* (published shortly before his own edition of Milton in 1784), where it is said of an unearthly sound issuing from a cave—

'But grinding through some *scrannel* frame
Creaked from the bony lungs of death.'

No doubt Langhorne copied the word from *Lycidas*, since he is known to have been a student of Milton, and a translator of the *Epitaphium Damonis* and the Italian poems. In the Lancashire dialect it means 'thin' or 'meagre,' and it is a question whether Milton was aware of its existence there, or whether he coined it to express the sound, after the analogy of *crane*, *screech* (G. *schreien*), &c. The former hypothesis is more probable, considering the extent of his information, and the improbability of his indulging in a license, which would be questionable in point of taste, and of which there would be no other instance in his poems. It has also been suggested that the word may be connected with *cranny*, and that if so, it would well express the squeaking noise produced from a pipe not perfectly air-tight. But this is doubtful.

125] Cf. *Epit. Dam.* 67, where the sheep mourn in sympathy, 'inque suum convertunt ora magistrum.'

are not fed] Cf. *Reason of Church Gov.*, ad fin., 'The swelling mood of a proud clergy, who will not serve or feed your souls with spiritual food.' One of the objections to the *King's Letters* of 1623 (see on *l.* 119) ran thus—'This is the way to starve souls, by confining them to one meal a day, or at best by giving them only a mess of milk for their supper' (in reference to the substitution of catechising for afternoon sermons). To which it was answered that 'milk is best for babes, which make up more than a moiety of every congregation.'

126] Peck compares Dante, *Paradiso*, Canto 29—

'Sì che le pecorelle, che non sanno,
Tornan dal pasco *pasciute di vento.*'

Cf. Virg. *Georg.* iii. 504 (of the cattle-plague), 'imaque longo Ilia singultu tendunt,' and the λιγξ κενή in Thucydides' description of the pestilence at Athens (ii. 49). Here of course there is direct allusion to the 'windy' words of the preacher, which may be illustrated by the Homeric phrase ἀνεμώλια βάζειν (*Il.* iv. 355), and the German *windreden* ' to talk vainly.'

For the 'rank mist' cf. Song of

Rot inwardly, and foul contagion spread ;
Beside what the grim wolf with privy paw
Daily devours apace, and nothing said.'

the Priest of Pan in Fletcher's *Faithful Shepherdess*—

'Mists unsound,
Damps and vapours fly apace,
Hovering o'er the wanton face
Of these pastures, where they come
Striking dead both bud and bloom.'

127] Milton may here have remembered Lucretius, vi. 1129 (of a vitiated atmosphere)—

' Et cum spirantes mixtos hinc *ducimus auras*,
Illa quoque in corpus pariter *sorbere necessest* ;'

also *ib.* 1235—

'nullo cessabant tempore a pisci
Ex aliis alios avidi *contagia morbi*.'

Becon in his *Supplication* uses similar language of popish pastors, 'Instead of thy blessed communion they feed thy sheep with vile stinking devilish masses ; and into these unwholesome and pestilent pastures they drive the sheep.'

128] Those who with Pearce and Newton believe Abp. Laud to be the 'wolf' here alluded to may compare the continuation of the passage just quoted—'and if any refuse to taste of these pestilent poisons, him they accite to appear before that *great wolf* [Bp. Gardiner], whose lips are full of deadly poison.' Reasons against this interpretation will be found in Appendix II.; here it may be noticed that the simile of wolves and sheep assumes three distinct forms in the New Testament—(1) *the wolf in sheep's clothing* (Matt. vii. 15), who enters the fold under false pretences ; (2) *the shepherd* who for his rapacity is said to devour the sheep (Acts xx. 29) ; (3) *the real wolf*, prowling outside the fold and seeking an entrance. The last appears to be the one here intended.

privy paw] So Diggon in Spenser's 9th Eclogue, *l.* 160, designates popish priests as wolves '*privily* prolling to and froe.' 'Privy' as an adjective, though not used elsewhere by Milton, was common in his time, and occurs in the Bible and Apocrypha (Ezek. xxi. 14; Susanna, 18; Bel and Dragon, 13, 21); also in the Litany, 'privy conspiracy.' Bacon in his *Essay on Building* speaks of 'privy lodgings and privy galleries.'

129] The spelling 'sed' of the MS. (cf *L'Allegro*, 101), altered to 'said' in ed. 1638, was replaced in the editions of 1645 and 1673. Warton in his *History of English Poetry* observes that in the Elizabethan period the spelling of final syllables was changed to satisfy the eye as well as the ear. Hence in Spenser we find such forms as 'bight,' 'spight,' to rime with 'delight,' 'dore' with 'restore,' &c., &c. In the MS. of *Lycidas* the last word of *l.* 193 is written 'blew' for the same reason, and in the 7th Sonnet 'yeere' and 'neere' are made to rime with 'careere.' Even in Pope's *Essay on Man*, 148 (ed. 1751), *sour* is spelt 'sowr' to rime with 'pow'r.' In the present passage some later editors, in ignorance of this custom, or mistaking the *f* for *ſ*, altered 'sed' to 'fed,' to the destruction of the sense. 'Nothing' was also changed to 'little' in 1638, but replaced in the next edition. On the facts of the case see Appendix II.

But that two-handed engine at the door   130
Stands ready to smite once, and smite no more.'
Return, Alpheüs, the dread voice is past

130] If the 'wolf' is not any individual but a system, neither is the 'two-handed engine' the axe by which Laud was to lose his head; an event which no one could easily have predicted in 1637. Milton is merely using the familiar simile of 'the axe laid to the root of the tree' (Matt. iii. 10), which denotes a thorough and sweeping reformation. Elsewhere he speaks more explicitly of 'the axe of God's reformation hewing at the old and hollow trunk of papacy,' and of the duty of cutting away 'the noisome and diseased tumour of prelacy;' here he names neither institution precisely, but alludes in general terms to the religious corruptions of the age and their speedy abolition; —'it is near, even at the doors' (Matt. xxiv. 33).

Two other interpretations may be dismissed as improbable—(1) that the 'engine' is the drawn sword of St. Michael standing on the Mount (l. 161), and the 'wolf' Satan; (2) that it refers to the executioner Death with his scythe. Warburton supposes that 'St. Peter's sword is turned into the two-handed sword of romance,' and compares *P. L.* vi. 251; but this idea was probably suggested by the identity of the epithet 'two-handed' in that passage, with which the present has nothing else in common. Keightley compares the ἀμφιδέξιον σίδηρον of Eurip. *Hippol.* 780.

engine] (*ingenium*) commonly denotes a machine more or less elaborately constructed. In *P. L.* B. vi. the term is often used of artillery in war (cf. Ezek. xxvi. 9); Butler in *Hudibras* applies it also to a telescope, a fiddle, and to edged tools; horses are called 'live engines,' according to a theory that they are machines made by geometry. Its application to a mere instrument wielded by the hand, as here, is less frequent. Cf. Pope, *Rape of the Lock*, iii. 132—

'he takes the *scissars* and extends
The little *engine* on his fingers' ends.'

131 smite no more] Newton compares 1 Sam. xxvi. 8. The blow is to be sudden and decisive.

132] As the return from the former digression (*l.* 85) was marked by the invocation of Arethusa, so now the poet addresses Alpheus, her legendary lover (Moschus, *Id.* 7; Ovid, *Met.* v. 576 foll.) The stern invective, which had scared away the pastoral Muse, is now over, and Milton reverts lovingly and enthusiastically to a strain more congenial to his feelings. Scott in his *Critical Essays* finds fault with the following lines, chiefly on the ground that 'too many flowers are specified, and spring flowers are injudiciously blended with summer ones—the primrose, cowslip, &c., with the pink and rose.' Milton at least must have thought otherwise, for no passage in the whole poem has been so carefully retouched as this (see Various Readings). Masson, vol. i. p. 614 note, remarks, 'Milton hovered over this passage with fastidious fondness, touching every colour and fitting every word, till he brought it to its present perfection of beauty.' Of these two pieces of criticism *utrum mavis accipe!*

t'e **dread voice, &c.]** a passing

That shrunk thy streams ; return, Sicilian Muse,
And call the vales, and bid them hither cast
Their bells, and flowerets of a thousand hues.   135
Ye valleys low, where the mild whispers use
Of shades, and wanton winds, and gushing brooks ;
On whose fresh lap the swart-star sparely looks :

recognition of the superior power of Christianity over Paganism. The voice of St. Peter represents that of Christ himself speaking to the Church. Dunster cites Psalm civ. 6.

133] The 'Sicilian Muse' is the muse of Theocritus. Cf. Virg. *Ecl.* iv. 1 ; vi. 1. Bion and Moschus make a similar acknowledgment in Σικελὸν μέλος and Σικελικὰ Μοῖσαι. So Milton speaks of 'Himerides Nymphæ' and 'Sicelicum carmen' in the opening lines of the *Epitaphium Damonis*. It may be observed that Theocritus himself does not thus localise his muse ; he simply says ἄρχετε βωκολικᾶς, Μῶσαι φίλαι, ἄρχετ' ἀοιδᾶς. In Virgil the 'Sicilian' epithet implies a professed imitation of his Greek original ; with Milton it has become a general literary designation of pastoral poetry. (See Introduction.)

134 hither] i.e. on the hearse of Lycidas, as if his body were actually present (*ll.* 152, 153). On the custom of pinning verses to the hearse see note on *l.* 151.

136 use] = 'haunt.' Cf. Spenser, *F. Q.* B. VI., *Introd.* ii. 17, 'where never foot did *use*.' May translates Virg. *Georg.* iii. 418, 'Snakes that *use* within the house for shade' ('tecto *adsuetus* coluber'), quoted by Newton and Todd. The reverse order of meaning appears in 'wont,' which first signified 'dwelling' (G. *wohnen*), and then 'custom.' Cf. *P. L.* vii. 457, 'the wild beast where he *wons*.' Both verb and noun in this sense are common in Spenser. Compare ἤθεα ('haunts'), from ἔθος ('custom'), in Homer and Hesiod.

137 wanton winds] i.e. roving at will (see Appendix I.). Cf. *Arcades*, 47, 'wanton windings ;' *P. L.* ix. 517, 'many a wanton wreath.' Taken in its usual sense, the epithet may remind us here of the mythological amours of the winds with nymphs, such as that of Boreas with Orithyia (Ovid, *Met.* vi. 677 ; Plato, *Phædrus*, c. 1), and of Zephyrus with Aurora (*L'Allegro*, 19).

138 swart-star] the dog-star, 'Sirius ardor' (Virg. *Æn.* x. 273), alluding to the effect of heat on vegetation. Newton quotes Hor. *Od.* III. xii. 9, 'Te flagrantis atrox hora Caniculæ Nescit tangere ;' he does not say (as Warton alleges) that 'Milton had an eye to Horace here,' but merely compares the two passages. For 'swart' (O. E. *sweart*, G. *schwartz*) cf. *Comus*, 436 ; Shaksp. 1 *Hen. VI.* i. 2, 'I was black and *swart* before ;' Keats, *Endymion*, B. ii., 'some *swart* abysm.' Cædmon speaks of 'the *swart* hell, a land void of light and full of flame.'

sparely] the original MS. reading restored by Milton's own hand. (See list of Various Readings.)

The simple occurrence of the word 'looks' is perhaps hardly sufficient to justify Warton's conjecture that the astrological 'aspect' of a star is here intended ; yet such an allusion is possible (cf. *Arcades*, 51 ;

LYCIDAS. 77

Throw hither all your quaint-enamelled eyes,
That on the green turf suck the honied showers,   140
And purple all the ground with vernal flowers.

P. L. vi. 313). We know that astrology was much in vogue at this period, the most famous professor of the art being W. Lilly, who died in 1681, and was satirised in *Hudibras* under the name of Sidrophel.

139 quaint] in its usual Miltonic sense of 'curious' or 'fantastic.' Cf. *P. L.* ix. 35; *Arc.* 47; *Od. Nat.* 194. In Spenser, *F. Q.* IV. vii. 45, 'usage quaint' = odd behaviour. As applied to character it means 'ingenious' or 'artful.' Shaksp. 2 *Hen. VI.* iii. 2, 'how quaint an orator you are;' *Merch. of Ven.* iii. 4, 'quaint lies.' Its primary meaning is 'neat' (of dress or personal appearance), as in *Much Ado*, iii. 4, 'quaint graceful fashions,' from the Old French *coint*, which is usually considered to represent the Latin *comptus*. Cf. Du Cange, *Gloss.* s.v., 'Galli *coints* dicebant cultos, elegantes, *comptos.*' But Wedgwood properly follows Diez in deriving it from *cognitus*, the idea being that of 'amenities arising from civilised intercourse.' The various stages of derivation are clearly shown in the case of *acquaint* from *adcognitare*, which latter word became in Old French *acointer*, and then *ac(c)ointer*, whence followed in due order *acoint*, *acqueynt*, and *acquaint*. Compare the different senses of 'couth' and 'uncouth' (*l.* 186 and note).

enamelled] painted as on enamel, a favourite word with the older poets. Cf. *P. L.* iv. 149; ix. 525; *Arc.* 84. Chaucer, *Assembly of Ladies*, 'flowers of right fine enamaile.' Drayton, *Muses' Elysium*, 'the enameled bravery of the beauteous spring.'

140 honied] like its Latin equivalent, *mellitus*, is one of the many instances of adjectives formed with the termination of a past participle, without the intervention of an actually existing verb. Milton seems to have been very fond of this formation. Cf. 'mitred,' *supra*, 112. The *Nativity Ode* alone contains seven or eight examples, as 'helmed,' 'sworded,' 'mooned,' &c. It is therefore strange that Dr. Johnson, writing in 1780, should condemn the practice in Gray's *Ode to Spring* as unscholarlike, or speak of it as having then but *lately* arisen. Peck also is mistaken in his mention of 'honied' and 'roseate' among the new words coined by Milton, for the former occurs in Shakspere, *Hen. V.* i. 1 ('honeyed sentences'), and in P. Fletcher's *Piscatory Eclogues*, iii. 14 ('thy honied tongue'), the latter in Drayton's *Muses' Elysium* ('roseate anadem'), in Marlow's *Translation of Ovid Eleg.* iv. ('roseate buds'), and in a poem ascribed to Sir W. Raleigh, *The Shepherd and the Flowers*, written about 1590.

141 purple] usually 'empurple,' *P. L.* iii. 364. The uncompounded verb occurs *P. L.* vii. 30. Cf. *Purple Island*, x. 81, '*Purpling* the scarlet cheek with fiery red.' Here, like *purpureus*, it denotes any bright colour, from a dazzling white (Hor. *Od.* IV. i. 10) to a deep red (Virg. *Æn.* ix. 349). Cf. *P. L.* iv. 764, 'his purple wings;' Spenser, *F. Q.* V. A. 16, 'the morrow next appeared with purple haire;' Gray, *Ode on Poesy*, 'the purple light of love' (Virgil's 'lumen juventæ purpureum,' *Æn.* i. 594).

Bring the rathe primrose that forsaken dies,
The tufted crow-toe, and pale jessamine,

142] Milton may or may not have remembered the list of flowers in Spenser, *Ecl.* iv. 136 foll., of which Mr. Bowles remarks that 'here is an undoubted imitation,' but he was certainly quite capable of inventing the following description for himself. Many instances of a similar enumeration occur in the classics, e.g. the elegy of Rufinus in the Greek Anthology, beginning πέμπω σοί, 'Ροδόκλεια, τόδε στέφος, &c. (where the κυαναυγὲς ἴον is named among others), and the list of flowers gathered by Proserpine and her maidens in Ovid, *Fast.* iv. 435 foll. When strewn upon the hearse each had its own fancied significance:—

'Here fresh roses lie,
Whose ruddy blushes modest thoughts descry.
The spotless lillies shew his pure intent;
The flaming marigolds his zeale present;
The purple violets his noble minde,
Degenerate never from his princely kinde;
And last of all the hyacinths we throw,
On which are writ the letters of our woe' (*l.* 106 note).

(*Elegy on Edward, son of Lord Stafford,* by Sir J. Beaumont.) Cf. *Purple Island,* ix. 319, 'And strewed with dainty flowers the lowly hearse.'

rathe] (O. E. *hræð*), 'early;' one of the really antiquated words in *Lycidas* (see on *l.* 189). Spenser has 'too rathe,' *F. Q.* III. iii. 28; 'rather (= earlier) lambs,' *Ecl.* xii. 98. Cf. Wither, *Shepheard's Hunting,* 4th Ecl. (1614), 'so rathe a song.' Warton quotes 'the rathe and timely primrose' from *England's Helicon* (1614). Dryden gives 'rathe ripe' as the translation of *precia* (Virg. *Georg.* ii. 95), which Servius explains by *præcoquæ,* 'early ripe.' Trench (*English Past and Present,* p. 98), lamenting the loss of this word, observes that it is 'embalmed in the *Lycidas* of Milton;' he also quotes an instance of the superlative 'rathest' in Bp. Sanderson's Sermons. It is worth noticing that *rathe* is still a common word for *early* in certain districts of South Wales.

forsaken] The first reading 'unwedded,' followed by the somewhat obscure line, 'Coloring the pale cheek of uninjoy'd love,' contained an allusion to the fabled amours of the Sun with certain flowers, and was doubtless suggested by the passage in Shakspere's *Winter's Tale,* iv. 4—

'*pale* primroses
That die *unmarried,* ere they can behold
Bright Phœbus in his strength;—
a malady
Most incident to maids.'

But no such idea is involved in the epithet as it now stands, which merely suggests the modest nature of the flower, blooming in retired spots, and often fading unnoticed.

143 foll.] See original reading, and cf. Quarles' *Emblems,* v. 2—

'The *purple vi'let* and the pale-fac'd lily,
The *pansy* and the organ *columbine,*
The flow'ring thyme, the gilt-breast *diaffodilly,*
The lowly *pink,* the lofty eglantine;
The blushing *rose,* the queen of flowers and best
Of Flora's beauty; but above the rest
Let *Jesse's* sov'reign flower perfume my qualming breast.'

LYCIDAS.

> The white pink, and the pansy freaked with jet,
> The glowing violet, 145
> The musk-rose, and the well-attired woodbine,
> With cowslips wan that hang the pensive head,
> And every flower that sad embroidery wears;
> Bid amaranthus all his beauty shed,
> And daffadillies fill their cups with tears, 150

The last is a play upon 'jessamine,' the real etymology of which is the Persian *jásmin*, 'fragrant.' The 'crowtoe' is perhaps the same as 'crowfoot,' a ranunculaceous plant, the name being applied to those species which have divided leaves. It is also called the 'kingcup.' Spens. *Ecl.* iv. 138 (Latham's *Johns. Dict.* s. v.). Richardson identifies it with the hyacinth, the 'sad flower, &c.' of the first draft, which was probably discarded because of the previous allusion to the same story in *l.* 106. A simple enumeration of the flowers is now substituted for the learned descriptions originally introduced. Moreover, three additional flowers—jessamine, pink, and musk-rose—are put in the place of the one (*narcissus*) which is lost.

144] Cf. *Comus*, 851. The 'pansy' is the flower of thought (*pensée*), as Ophelia says in *Hamlet*, iv. 5; it is also called 'love-in-idleness' (*Mids. N. Dream*, ii. 1), and commonly 'heartsease.'

freaked] = 'freckled,' Gael. *bréac*. Cf. Thomson, *Winter*, 826, 'freaked with many a mingled hue.' *Fraknes* in Chaucer = freckles.

145] Plumptre translates ἴων κυανανγὲς ἄνθος from Rufinus, quoted on *l.* 142 above.

146 well-attired woodbine] altered from 'garish columbine.' 'Garish' now occurs only in *Il Penseroso*, 141. Keightley compares Cowper, *Task*, 167, 'Meze- reon too. Though leafless, *well-attired*.'

148 embroidery] from Old French *broder*, to ornament with needle-work (Gael. *brod*, a needle); whence the Low Latin *brodare* = 'acu pingere,' Ducange, *Gloss.* In *P. L.* iv. 700, it is used to describe a field set with flowers. Cf. Chaucer, *Prologue to Cant. Tales* (of the Squire)—

> '*Embrouded* was he as it were a mede,
> Alle ful of freshe floures white and rede.'

The usual derivation from *border* is probably incorrect. Wedgwood, however, considers *brod* and *bord* to be identical, both meaning the extremity of a thing. He observes that the Icelandic *brydda* signifies both 'to sharpen' and 'to sew on an edging.' The first reading, 'sorrow's liverie,' is illustrated by Todd from Wither's *Juvenilia* and Habington's *Castara.* Cf. Fletcher, *Purple Island*, viii. 5, 'night's sad livery,' also *L'Allegro*, 62. In *P. L.* iv. 599, Milton speaks of the 'sober livery' of twilight.

149 amaranthus] (ἀμάραντος), the unfading (1 Peter i. 4), an emblem of immortality. It is placed in Eden 'fast by the tree of life,' *P. L.* iii. 354.

150] Keats, *Endymion*, B. iv., 'brimming the water-lily cups with tears.' 'Daffodil' is properly 'affodil' from ἀσφόδελος through Med. Latin

To strew the laureate herse where Lycid lies.—
For so, to interpose a little ease,
Let our frail thoughts dally with false surmise;
Ay me ! whilst thee the shores and sounding seas

affodillus; the origin of the *d* is doubtful. It is really a species of narcissus. The form 'daffodilly' occurs in the Song to Pan in Fletcher's *Faithful Shepherdess*; Spenser, *F. Q.* III. iv. 29; *Ecl.* iv. 60; 'daffadowndillies' in *Ecl.* iv. 140.

151] 'The *herse* was a platform, decorated with black hangings, and containing an effigy of the deceased. Laudatory verses were attached to it with pins, wax, or paste.' (Stanley, *Memorials of Westminster Abbey*, p. 341.) Cf. King's *Elegy on Donne*—

Each quill can drop his tributary verse,
And pin it like the hatchments to the herse.'

For the *word* see Appendix I.

laureate] 'decked with laurel' (*laureatus*), cf. *l.* 1. Plumptre's rendering, δαφνίναν, would mean 'made of laurel' (*laureus*), a sense in which 'laureate' is sometimes used, e.g. 'laureat wreath,' *Sonnet* xvi. 19. *Laureatus* is applied both to persons and things, but usually to the former, as a mark of honour; hence the title 'poeta laureatus,' first *officially* conferred on B. Jonson in 1619.

Lycid] Cf. Keats, *Sonnet* xi.—

'Of fair-haired Milton's eloquent distress,
And all his gentle love for *Lycid* drowned.'

The older poets were fond of shortening classical names thus. Chaucer has Creysyd, Pandare, Adon, &c.; in Surrey we find Arge, Ide, Sichee, &c.; in Spenser, Archimag, Acidale, Melibee, &c. Milton does not so frequently avail himself of this license, excepting in a few commoner forms, such as Dian, Hecat', Ind, &c.; otherwise the name 'Erymanth' in *Arcades*, 100, is almost a solitary instance.

152] 'For' connects this line with the preceding mention of the hearse of Lycidas; '*for* let us suppose his body to be lying here before us, though really it is far away.' The structure of the next sentence (placing a semicolon after 'surmise') must be as follows: 'Let our thoughts dally, &c. [principal verb], *while* the seas wash thee far away, where'er thy bones are hurled—*whether* beyond the Hebrides (where thou visitest, &c.), *or whether* thou sleepest, &c. (where the great vision looks towards Namancos and Bayona).' On the person addressed in *l.* 163 see note there.

153 **dally**] i.e. 'play' or 'trifle,' akin to G. *tändeln* and *dahlen*, to trifle. Cf. Shaksp. *Hamlet*, v. 2, 'you do but dally.' In the Apocryphal Book of Wisdom, xii. 26, God's judgments upon the Canaanites are spoken of as 'that correction wherein he *dallied* with them . . . as children without the use of reason.' Skeat connects *dally* with M.E. *dalien*, 'to be foolish.'

surmise] here = 'fancy,' usually 'conjecture.'

154 **Ay me!**] See on *l.* 56.

Scott, *Critical Essays*, notices the following lines as an instance of poetical imagination of the right kind, which 'should not produce impossible fictions, but explore real existence, and select from it circumstances as occasion requires.'

Wash far away,—where'er thy bones are hurled, 155
Whether beyond the stormy Hebrides,
Where thou perhaps under the whelming tide
Visitest the bottom of the monstrous world;
Or whether thou, to our moist vows denied,
Sleepest by the fable of Bellerus old, 160

the shores—wash, &c.] This expression, though strange, is not the result of oversight, since Milton deliberately substituted 'shoars' for 'floods' in his MS. The obvious meaning is that the corpse visited different parts of the *coast* in its wanderings, and was not out at sea all the time. The word *shore* does however literally mean 'that which *divides* the water from the land,' and therefore includes the portion sometimes covered by the tide. So Celsus defines *litus*, 'quousque maximus fluctus a mari pervenit.' Newton cites Virg. Æn. vi. 362, 'Nunc me fluctus habet, versantque in litore venti,' which is a case in point only on the assumption that the latter clause cannot mean 'cast up *on* the shore;' a sense which Heyne and Conington both adopt, comparing Eur. *Hec.* 28, κεῖμαι δ' ἐπ' ἀκταῖς, ἄλλοτ' ἐν πόντου σάλῳ. (*In* with the ablative occasionally denotes motion, as in Phædrus, *Fab.* v. i. 15, 'in conspectu meo audet venire.')

155 far away] here (according to Newton) = '*at* a great distance,' not *to* it. Keightley notes the expression as 'ambiguous.' It probably means 'far from the scene of the shipwreck.'

156 whether, &c.] Cf. Ode on *Death of a Fair Infant*, 38 foll.; Aristoph. *Nubes*, 269 foll., referred to on *l.* 50.

157] The first reading, 'humming,' for 'whelming,' was inappropriate to the case of a dead man, who could not hear the sound of the waves. But Shakspere commits the same error when he makes Pericles (iii. 1) apostrophise his dead queen with the words, 'And *humming* water must o'erwhelm thy corpse.' Warton compares Virg. *Georg.* iv. 365, where Aristæus, in his mother's ocean cave, is said to be 'ingenti motu stupefactus aquarum.'

158 monstrous] i. e. 'full of monsters,' the proper sense of the Latin ending -*osus*, as in *saxosus*, &c. *Monstruosus* itself, however, never bears this meaning, e.g. 'monstruosa bestia,' &c.; and Milton elsewhere employs 'monstrous' in its usual acceptation, *P. L.* ii. 625; *Comus*, 605, &c. Here he seems to have remembered Hor. *Od.* I. iii. 18, and Virg. Æn. vi. 729. Cf. Hom. *Od.* iii. 158, μεγακήτεα πόντον.

159 moist vows] i.e. 'vows accompanied with tears' (Warton). *Vota humida* would be a correct expression in Latin, though it does not seem to occur. Martial, *Epigr.* x. lxxviii. 8, has 'udo gaudio,' meaning 'joy mingled with weeping.' Plumptre's translation, ὑγραῖς εὐχαῖς, is questionable.

160 fable of Bellerus] = 'fabled abode of Bellerus' (*sedes fabulosa*); something like 'fabulæ Manes,' Hor. *Od.* I. iv. 16 (for *Manes fabulosi*), 'the ghosts of olden story.' The name is coined from Bellerium, now the Land's End. Cf. Cowley, *Plantarum Liber*, vi., 'Belerii extremis a cornibus Orcadas usque;' Pope, *Windsor Forest*, 315, 'From old

> Where the great Vision of the guarded Mount
> Looks toward Namancos and Bayona's hold :—
> Look homeward, Angel, now, and melt with ruth,

Belerium to the northern main.' The original reading was 'Corineus,' whom Milton mentions in his *History of Britain*, B. i., as a giant who came over with Brute the Trojan, and from whom Cornwall took its name, being 'assigned to him by lot,' or, as Drayton says (*Polyolb.* 1st Song), given him for his victory over Gogmagog the Cornish giant. The change of reading may have been made for rhythmical reasons, as 'Bēllērus' runs more smoothly in the line than 'Cŏrīnĕus.'

A writer in the *Edinburgh Review*, 1821, has the following remarks on Milton's treatment of early British legends :—'Milton was perhaps the first who dared disavow his belief of the legends which for centuries had been placed at the head of the early history of England. [See *Hist. of Britain*, B. i.] Yet he deigns to relate them, because the very belief in them was characteristic of a nation ; because they might contain some traces of ancient tradition, and be an evidence of manners, if not of events ; and lastly as themes for the poet, on which he had himself once meditated to build a monument to the glory of his country.' [See *Epist. ad Mansum*, l. 78; *Epit. Dam.* l. 162.]

161] The 'guarded (fortified) Mount' is a steep rock opposite Marazion near Penzance, accessible from the land at low water. On it are the ruins of a fortress and a monastery, with a church dedicated to St. Michael ; at the summit is a craggy seat called St. Michael's chair, in which several apparitions of the archangel are reported to have been seen ; hence the 'great Vision' in the text. Carew, in his *Survey of Cornwall*, alludes to the Mount as a favourite resort of pilgrims, quoting the lines—

'Who knows not Mighel's Mount and Chaire,
The pilgrim's holy vaunt ?'

Cf. Spenser, *Ecl.* vii. 41—
'St. Michael's Mount who does not know,
That guards the westerne coast ?'

162] The question as to the locality of Namancos puzzled commentators not a little, until Todd (1809) referred to Mercator's Atlas of 1636, in which the place is clearly marked rather to the east of Cape Finisterre, with the Castle of Bayona on the south. Namancos also appears in Ojea's map of Galicia (1650), but seems to have been afterwards omitted, as it is not found in Nolin's map (1762), nor in that of Lopez (1784), nor in the *Atlas Nacional de España* of 1838. Todd in his edition of 1801 had suggested Numantia, and Dunster, adopting this view, took Bayona to be the French Bayonne ; but it is plain that no one could 'look towards' both these places at once in a direct line from St. Michael's Mount. Cf. Drayton, *Polyolb.* 23rd Song—

'Then Cornwal creepeth out into the western maine,
As lying in her eye she pointeth still at Spaine.'

163] The obvious and striking contrast between the 'look homeward' of this line and the looking 'towards Namancos, &c.' of the one preceding clearly justifies Warton's supposition that St. Michael, and not Lycidas, is the person here

And, O ye dolphins, waft the hapless youth.

addressed. Still, the arguments in favour of the contrary interpretation ought to be fairly stated. It has been objected that if a full stop be placed at 'surmise,' the present line is required to complete the sentence beginning at 'whilst thee, &c.,' which would otherwise be unfinished, and of which Lycidas is the subject throughout; and that, even with the semicolon there (see on *l.* 152), St. Michael's apparition is merely introduced parenthetically, as part of a local description, and never directly apostrophised. This is perhaps strictly true; but a poet is not always bound by the strict laws of grammatical construction, and the sudden turn of address from Lycidas to the archangel (who is now a prominent figure in the description) strikes powerfully upon the reader's imagination. Another argument (which at first sight appears plausible) is founded upon the coincidence of the present passage and of *ll.* 183 foll. in structure, language, and sentiment, with certain lines in the 1st *Eclogue* of Sannazaro (*circ.* 1520), in which a drowned man is thus addressed by his mourning friends:

'At tu, *sive* altum felix colis æthera,
    seu jam
Elysios inter Manes, &c. . . .
Aspice nos mitisque veni, *tu numen
    aquarum
Semper eris, semper lætum* piscantibus *omen.*'

But even admitting, as we surely may (cf. especially *l.* 184), that Milton had the above passage generally in view, we need not assume that he copied his original with such exactness, as to make the subject of his 'look homeward' correspond with that of 'aspice' in Sannazaro. We do not however agree

with Warton's further objection, that an address to the departed spirit would be in itself inappropriate. A few instances out of many will suffice to show that the sentiment is both natural and common. Spenser in his *Elegy on Sir P. Sidney* invokes the 'happy sprite' to 'look down awhile' upon his friends; Donne makes a similar appeal to the soul of Lord Harrington, and Habington entreats the spirit of George, Earl of Surrey, to 'look down with propitious eyes and smile upon this sacrifice.' The language of Cowley in his *Death of Hervey* still more closely resembles that of Milton, when he imagines 'the glorious saints' as beholding their friends 'with holy *pity*;' and Young, in his *Night Thoughts*, says of the dead, 'They live . . . and from an eye of tenderness let heavenly *pity* fall.'

ruth] Cf. Chaucer, *Troilus and Creyseyde*, 'have routh upon my pains;' Sidney, *Arcadia*, B. i. Ecl. 1, 'thou my dog whose *ruth* (pity for the flock) and valiant might, &c.' Primarily the word means 'sorrow,' from 'rue' (O. E. *hreów-an*, G. *reuen*). Cf. B. Jonson, *Epitaph on his Daughter*, 'her parents' ruth.' 'Pity and ruth' are joined in Milton's 9th *Sonnet, l* 8, and in Spenser, *F. Q.* I. vi. 12. For the verb in its secondary sense cf. Wyatt, 51st Psalm, '*rue* on me, Lord;' Watson (1593), 41st *Sonnet*, '*rew* and pittie my vexations.' 'Ruthful' occurs in Shaksp. 1 *Hen. VI.* v. 5, and elsewhere; 'rueful' and 'ruthless' still survive.

164] Richardson refers to Pausanias' statement about Palæmon, 'that a dolphin took him up and laid his body on the shore at Corinth, where he was deified' (cf.

Weep no more, woful shepherds, weep no more, 165
For Lycidas, your sorrow, is not dead,

ll. 183-185). Stories of the amiability of dolphins were common in ancient times. Besides the familiar legend of Arion (Herod. i. 24; Ov. *Fast*. ii. 105 foll.), we have the one quoted from Apion by Gellius, *Noct. Att.* vii. 8, of a dolphin who carried a boy on his back daily from Baiæ to Puteoli, and on the death of the boy pined away with grief. Pliny, *Nat. Hist.* ix. 8, describes the animal as 'maxime homini amicum' (cf. Arist. *De Animalibus*, ix. 35), and especially notices its care of its own species, when dead or wounded. Some of these tales about dolphins may (as Liddell and Scott suppose *s. v.* δελφίς) be due to the fact of their playing in stormy weather, and so warning mariners of danger; the 'curved back' (Ov. *l. c.* 137) might suggest the idea of carrying a burden. Cf. Shaksp. *Ant. and Cleop.* v. 2—

'his delights
Were dolphin-like; they showed
  his back above
The element they lived in.'

165-185] 'The common conclusion of a funeral elegy is the beatification of the deceased' (Scott, *Critical Essays*). Here the classical apotheosis forms an additional feature in the description (see on *l.* 183, and the concluding lines of the *Epit. Damonis*). What follows may be compared with Spenser, *Ecl.* xi. 169 foll.—

'Dido is dead, but unto heaven
  hent; . . .
She reignes a goddess now emong
  the saintes; . . .
There drinckes she nectar with
  ambrosia mixt, &c.'

Cf. Watson, *Eclogue on the Death of Meliæus* (Sir F. Walsingham), 1590—
'Injustlie judge we Melibœus' death,
  As though his worth was buried
  in his fate;
Now Melibœus in comparelesse
  place
Drinkes nectar, eates divine ambrosia.'

Contrast the sentiment of Moschus, *Epit. Bionis*, 112-141, of a portion of which we offer the following paraphrase: 'Alas! the herbs wither and grow again; while we the mighty and the wise, all speechless in the tomb, sleep the long endless slumber that knows no waking (ἀτέρμονα νήγρετον ὕπνον). . . . But tune thou thy lay before the queen of Hades, if haply thy music may win a guerdon for thee, and thou mayest return to earth once more.' On the other hand, see Virgil's apotheosis of Cæsar, under the name of Daphnis, *Ecl.* v. 56 foll., only observing that the glory which he reserves for an extraordinary hero, Milton, as a Christian, claims for all pious souls. For 'woful,' applied to persons, cf. Sidney's *Arcadia*, B. ii., 'the woeful Gynecia;' Daniel, *Civil Wars*, 'How many woeful maidens left to mourn!'

166 **your sorrow**] i.e. the object of your sorrow, *vester dolor*. Cf. Propert. I. xiv. 18, 'Illa etiam duris mentibus (potest) esse *dolor*.' So *mea desideria*, 'my love,' Cic. *Epist. Fam.*

not dead]. Cf. *Death of Fair Infant*, *l*. 29. Warton quotes from the *Lay of Clorinda* (attributed to Spenser) the lines beginning 'Ah no, it is not dead ne can it die.' Cf. *Epitaph on Sir W. Drury*, by Barnabe Ritche, in the *Paradise of Dayntie Devises*, 1579:—

LYCIDAS.

Sunk though he be beneath the watery floor.
So sinks the day-star in the ocean bed,
And yet anon repairs his drooping head,
And tricks his beams, and with new-spangled ore   170

'Your Drury is not dead!
He liveth he amongst the blessed
route. . . .
Wherefore, you worthy wightes,
leave of to wayle.'

167 floor] (G. *Flur*) is any level surface (*æquor*). Cf. *Arcadia*, B. i., 'the morning did strew roses and violets in the heavenly floor.' Schiller, in his poem entitled *Das Ideal und das Leben*, has 'des Lichtes Fluren,' 'fields of light.'

168] The 'day-star' may possibly, as Newton thinks, be the sun, which is called the 'diurnal star' in *P. L.* x. 1069. Cf. Pindar, *Olymp.* i. 9, μήκεθ' ἁλίου σκόπει ἄλλο θαλπνότερον...ἄστρον; Ovid, *Fast.* vi. 718, where 'stella serena' is said of Phœbus; also *Met.* i. 429; Tibull. II. i. 47, where 'sidus' is similarly used. The chief advantage of this interpretation would be to save Milton from the astronomical blunder involved in making the same planet a morning and an evening star in one day; but here, as in *l.* 30 (see note), he is most likely to have followed the usage of the ancients, who commonly speak of Lucifer and Hesperus in this way. Catullus, lxii. 34, describes the evening star as returning next morning, 'mutato nomine;' Horace, *Od.* II. ix. 10, measures a night's duration by the rising and setting of Hesperus; and Virgil, *Ecl.* viii. 17 and 30, makes Lucifer and Hesperus appear during the same day. Moreover, the present passage is evidently copied from Virg. *Æn.* viii. 589, 'Qualis ubi Oceani perfusus Lucifer unda, &c.,' compared with the original in Hom. *Il.* v. 6, thus translated by Lord Derby:—

'like autumn's star, that brightest shines
When newly risen from his ocean bath.'

Compare also the closely similar language in Giles Fletcher's *Christ's Triumph after Death*, ll. 89 foll.—

'So fairest Phosphor, the bright morning-star,
But newly washed in the green element,
Before the drowsy night is half aware,
Shooting his flaming locks with dew besprent,
Springs lively up into the orient.'

169 anon] = *in one* (moment), immediately. The word is common in Shakspere; see especially the scene at the Boar's Head Tavern, 1 *Hen. IV.* ii. 4. It occurs twice only in the authorised version of the Bible, Matt. xiii. 20, Mark i. 30.

repairs] 'refreshes,' from *reparare*, to get a fresh supply in place of what is lost or damaged. Hor. *Od.* IV. vii. 13, 'Damna tamen celeres *reparant* cælestia lunæ.' The line in Gray's *Bard*, *l.* 137 (of the sun), 'to-morrow he repairs his golden flood,' quoted by Warton, is probably a reminiscence of Milton.

170 tricks] sets in order, adorns. Cf. *Il Penseroso*, 123; Shaksp. *Merry W. of Windsor*, iv. 4, 'trickings for our fairies.' Todd on *Il Pens. l. c.* quotes from Sandys' *Travels*, B. i. (of a Turkish bride), 'they *trick* her in her richest ornaments.' (On the etymology and

LYCIDAS.

Flames in the forehead of the morning sky :
So Lycidas sunk low, but mounted high
Through the dear might of Him that walked the waves,
Where, other groves and other streams along,
With nectar pure his oozy locks he laves, 175

senses of the word see Appendix I.)

spangled] from Gaelic *spang*, a metal plate. Cf. Spenser, *F. Q.* IV. xi. 45, 'glittering spangs.' It is rather a favourite word with Milton (*P. L.* vii. 384, *Od. Nat.* 21, *Psalm* cxxxvi. 35, &c.); like *tinsel* (*Comus*, 877) and others, it has now lost somewhat of its dignity. See Trench, *Study of Words*, p. 52; *Eng. Past and Present*, p. 130. 'Spangled heavens' occurs in Addison's well-known paraphrase of the 19th Psalm.

ore] = 'golden radiance,' as in Keats' *Endymion*, B. ii., 'a golden splendour with quivering *ore*.' For '*ore*' in the distinctive sense of 'gold' (probably owing to an erroneous derivation from *aurum*) cf. *Comus*, 932; Shaksp. *Hamlet*, iv. 1, 'like some ore among a mineral of metals base.' It is applied to other metals, iron or copper, in *P. L.* xi. 570. The word properly signifies a *vein* of metal in the mine (Dutch *aare*, G. *ader*). P. Fletcher, *Purple Island*, ix. 251, has the line—
'And round about was writ in *golden ore*.'

171] Crashaw, *Weeper*, st. 2, 'Whatever makes Heaven's forehead fine.' Tennyson, *Pelleas and Etarre*, 'the virgin forehead of the dawn.' Cf. 'the eyelids of the day,' supr. *l.* 26, and see note there.

173] See Matth. xiv. 22-23. Warton aptly observes that this is 'a designation of our Saviour by a miracle which bears an immediate reference to the subject of the poem.'

174 **other groves**, &c.] i.e. in another and *a better* world. Todd comp. Drummond's *Mæliades*, *l.* 175—
'other hills and forrests, other towers,
Amazed thou find'st excelling our poor bowers.'
Cf. Italian poems, *Canzone*, *l.* 8, '*altri* rivi, *altri* lidi t' aspettan, &c., i.e. the streams and shores of his native land, as contrasted with those of Italy.

along] = beside, amidst, without the usual idea of *motion*. So in the *Circumcision Ode*, *l.* 4, 'sung your joy the clouds along.'

175] Cf. *Ode on Fair Infant*, 49, 'thy nectared head.' Nectar with ambrosia is said to have been used by way of ablution to preserve immortality, as well as for the food and drink of the gods. Hom. *Il.* xiv. 170; xix. 39. In *Comus*, 836 foll., the deification of Sabrina is effected by 'nectared lavers' and 'ambrosial oils.'

oozy locks] Since 'ooze' properly means moisture of any kind (O. E. *wos*, 'juice'), it would be possible to understand 'oozy' of the effect of the nectar, according to the common classical figure called *prolepsis*; like Virgil's 'spicula lucida tergunt,' i.e. 'they scour their lances *so as to make them* bright.' But as the word is generally, if not invariably, used of slime or mud, it probably here refers to the sea water which is washed away by the nectar, and may be compared with Hom. *Il.* xiv. *l. c.*,

LYCIDAS.

And hears the unexpressive nuptial song,
In the blest kingdoms meek of joy and love.
There entertain him all the saints above,
In solemn troops and sweet societies,
That sing, and singing in their glory move,   180
And wipe the tears for ever from his eyes.
Now, Lycidas, the shepherds weep no more ;
Henceforth thou art the Genius of the shore,

λύματα πάντα καθῆρεν. Cf. Pope, *Odyssey*, iv. 543, 'His oozy limbs.'

176 and hears] originally 'list'n-ing,' with an ellipse of the preposition, common in Elizabethan writers. Cf. Shaksp. *Macbeth*, ii. 2, 'listening their fear.'

unexpressive] not to be expressed, 'inenarrabile carmen,' *Od. Ad Patrem*, 37. Cf. *Od. Nat.* 116. Shakspere has 'plausive,' 'insuppressive,' 'directive,' &c., used passively for 'plausible,' &c. Newton instances 'the unexpressive she' (*As You Like It*, iii. 2). The grammatical terms 'derivative,' 'adjective,' &c., are also cases in point. For the 'nuptial song' Newton refers to Rev. xiv. 3, 4; the reference should rather be Rev. xix. 6, 7, the song at 'the marriage supper of the Lamb.'

177] This line was omitted, probably by a printer's error, in the edition of 1638; it is inserted in Milton's handwriting in his own copy of that edition, preserved in the Cambridge University Library. 'Meek,' i.e. peaceful, is a suitable epithet of 'kingdoms,' and need not, as Thyer supposes, be referred by transposition to 'joy and love.' Nor is this interpretation supported by the passage which Newton quotes from *P. L.* ix. 318, where the epithet 'domestic' belongs quite naturally to Adam as a loving spouse,

and does not require to be taken with 'care.'

178] Warton's remark that 'even here Milton does not make Lycidas an *angel*,' ought not to have been used by way of argument in support of his explanation of *l.* 163. One of Drummond's elegies is addressed 'to the *Angel Spirit* of the most excellent Sir Philip Sidney,' and the expression is amply justified by popular usage.

179] There is no necessary allusion in this line to the 'angelick system,' which is set forth with some minuteness in the *Reason of Church Government*, B. I. c. I. (cf. *P. L.* v. 601; xi. 80), as 'saints' and not angels are here specified. The Christian doctrine of the *Communion of Saints* needs no illustration.

181] Rev. vii. 17; xxi. 4; Isai. xxv. 8, where the act is attributed to God Himself.

183] See quotation from Sannazaro on *l.* 163, and cf. Blacklock's Monody, *Philanthes* :—

'Still he, the genius of our green retreat,
Shall with benignant care our labour cheer.'

Many will agree with Todd in wishing that 'after the sublime intimation of angels wiping the tears from the eyes of Lycidas [he] had not been converted into the classical

In thy large recompense, and shalt be good
To all that wander in that perilous flood.   185
Thus sang the uncouth swain to the oaks and rills,

Genius of the shore.' For although the individual Genius is a conception in many points similar to that of the guardian angel, the *Genius loci* can have no counterpart in modern religious belief, being a product of that localising tendency of Pagan theology which it was one special aim of Christianity to abolish (John iv. 21 foll.). The mention of him here serves, somewhat inartistically, to mark a return to the pastoral form in which the poem is chiefly set. Newton supposes an allusion to the story of Melicerta, told in the 6th book of Ovid's *Fasti*, and referred to by Virgil, *Georg.* i. 436; but the language in the text is perhaps hardly definite enough to make this reference certain.

184 in thy large recompense] i.e. 'by way of ample requital to thee (for thy sufferings).' The phrase is doubtful English, but it represents such Greek forms of expression as ὁ σὸς πόθος = 'regret for thee,' where the possessive stands for an oblique case of the personal pronoun. See note on *l.* 166.

shalt be good, &c.] Thyer compares Virg. *Ecl.* v. 64, 'Sis bonus o, felixque tuis,' addressed to the deified Daphnis.

185 perilous] pronounced as a dissyllable everywhere in Milton, except in *P. L.* ii. 420. Cf. Spenser, *F. Q.* II. vi. 38, 'that perlous shard;' Keats, *Endymion*, bk. iii., 'in perilous bustle.' Hence the colloquial form 'parlous,' Shaksp. *Mids. N. Dream*, iii. 1, 'a parlous fear,' especially in the sense of *alarmingly clever*, 'a parlous boy,' *K. Rich. III.* ii. 4.

186–194] 'The shepherd elegiast, who has not yet been formally introduced, is now set before us among his oaks and rills' (Scott, *Critical Essays*). Keightley, in his *Life and Opinions of Milton*, observes that these last eight lines form a perfect stanza in *ottava rima*, which is imitated by Mason in his *Musæus*.

186 uncouth] It is doubtful whether this word is to be taken in its literal sense of 'unknown' (O.E. *cúð*, p. part. of *cúnnan*), or in the usual modern acceptation of 'rude,' 'uncultivated.' The former would be a natural expression of a young poet just entering upon a career of fame (cf. *l.* 3 and note), but Milton does not seem to have used the term elsewhere of *persons* with this meaning. In *P. L.* ii. 407 Satan's journey towards this world is called 'his uncouth way,' and in vi. 361 'uncouth pain' means 'unusual.' Cf. Spenser, *F. Q.* I. xi. 20. In *P. L.* v. 98, and probably in *L'Allegro*, 5, this sense is combined with the secondary one of 'hideous,' to which the transition is complete in *S. A.* 333, where Manoah speaks of the prison at Gaza as 'this uncouth place.' The modern application to manners, from the idea of 'strange' or 'out of place,' is obvious and easy (see note on 'quaint,' *l.* 139). This and the following lines are thus imitated by M. Bruce in his *Daphnis* :—

'A *homely swain* tending his little flock,
Rude, yet a lover of the Muses' lore,
Chanted his *Doric strain* till close of day.'

While the still Morn went out with sandals gray;
He touched the tender stops of various quills,
With eager thought warbling his Doric lay;
And now the sun had stretcht out all the hills, 190
And now was dropped into the western bay.
At last he rose, and twitcht his mantle blue;
To-morrow to fresh woods, and pastures new.

187] Cf. *P. R.* iv. 426:—
'till morning fair
Went forth with pilgrim steps in
amice gray.'

188] A 'stop' is properly that which covers the ventholes in a flute or similar wind instrument; hence it is applied to the holes themselves. The best illustration is that quoted by Warton from *Hamlet*, iii. 2:—'Govern these ventages with your fingers and thumb. ... Look you, these are the *stops*.' Cf. *Comus*, 346, whence Collins took his 'oaten stop or pastoral song,' *Ode to Evening*, *l*. 1. The stops of an organ are only a more elaborate contrivance for applying the same principle to a number of pipes together; these are mentioned in *P. L.* xi. 561.

various quills] in allusion to the varied strains of the elegy (at *ll*. 76, 88, 113, 132, 165). This almost amounts to a recognition on the part of the poet of the irregularity of style, the mixture of different and even opposing themes, which some have censured as a defect. 'Quill' (L. *calamus*, G. *kiel*) is literally a reed-pipe. So Spenser, *Ecl.* vi. 67, speaks of the 'homely shepherd's quill;' Collins, *Superstitions of the Highlands*, 'thy Doric quill;' Fletcher, *Purple Island*, xi. 10, 'my oaten quill.' Johnson explains it of the *plectrum* with which the strings of the lyre were struck, in-stancing Dryden's *Virg. Æn.* vi. 646, 'his harmonious quill strikes seven distinguished notes' ('*pectine pulsat eburno*'); but this is not the usual sense of the word.

189 Doric lay] Δωρὶς ἀοιδά, Moschus, *Epit. Bionis*, 12, which is said to have perished with Bion. Here it stands for pastoral poetry, in reference to Theocritus (see on *ll.* 85, 133), not, as Newton supposes, to archaisms of language, which are not so frequent in this poem as to justify his remark quoted above on *l.* 4.

190 stretcht out, &c.] Milton has here added something of his own to the Virgilian picture in *Ecl.* i. 84, 'majoresque cadunt altis de montibus umbrae.'

192 twitcht] i.e. snatched up from where it lay beside him, κυάνεον δ' ἀφὰρ ἔλλαβεν εἷμα (Plumptre's Translation). Or, according to Keightley, 'drew tightly about him on account of the chillness of the evening.' In any case the word expresses haste, as if the setting sun had surprised him while 'eager' in his singing.

blue] the colour of a shepherd's dress, and the poet impersonates a shepherd (Hales, *Longer English Poems*). It is not probable that Milton meant anything more than this, though other explanations, more or less fanciful, have been offered.

193] Newton comp. Fletcher,

Purple Island, vi. 538, 'to-morrow shall ye feast in pastures new.' Professor Masson observes that this is 'a parting intimation that the imaginary shepherd is Milton himself, and that the poem is a tribute to his dead friend rendered passingly in the midst of other occupations' (see note on *l.* 1). It is better to refer these words to the projected Italian tour, with which his mind must now have been occupied, than to any political intentions at this time. Milton could not have foreseen the events of the next few years; and we know that the commotions which began in 1638–9 recalled him suddenly from abroad, where he had meant to stay for some time longer, and that the whole complexion of his future life was determined by them. It should be remembered that the next poem of any importance which he wrote was the *Paradise Lost*, begun probably in or about 1658, some two years before the Restoration.

APPENDIX I.

On the Etymology of some Words in the 'Lycidas.'

Rime (*l.* 11). It is, or ought to be, now generally known that the common spelling of this word (*rhyme*) owes its origin to a pedantic formation from ῥυθμός, made by those who claimed for it a Greek derivation, but that it is really the O.E. *rîm*, '*number*,' H.G. *reim*, Dutch *rijm*, &c., and that the true orthography is rime. Dr. Latham, in his new edition of Johnson's Dictionary, makes it a main ground of objection to this statement, that the Teutonic forms themselves may have been originally connected with ῥυθμός— a question obviously irrelevant to the matter in hand, which is simply to discover *how and whence the word first came into our language*. Nor is this a difficult task, since the older authorities all combine to prove that it was an English word from the first; for instance, in Havelok, the *Ormulum*, Shoreham, Hoccleve, and Horn (see Stratmann's Old English Dictionary), the spelling is always *rîm* or *rime*. We find indeed in Chaucer, Spenser, &c., a variant form *ryme*, but this is really of no importance, since *i* and *y* were constantly interchanged, as *fire* and *fyre*, *time* and *tyme*, &c.; and *ryme* may have been so spelt for the special reason of distinguishing it from *rime*, 'hoar-frost.' This evidence from the earlier orthography ought to be decisive; since an examination of the meaning and uses of the word leads to no certain conclusion either way. We know that it was at first a general term for 'verse' (as in the present line), and that after the introduction of blank verse in the 16th century it was applied to 'rhyming' poetry for the sake of distinction. But this general primary sense would be compatible either with a derivation from ῥυθμός or with one from *rîm*, since in both words the 'measured intervals' (*numeri*) of the verse form the leading idea. I had been unable to discover the exact date of the introduction of the *h* into the word *rhyme*, but since writing the first draft of this note my attention has been directed to a letter from Mr. F. J. Furnivall in *Notes and Queries*, Nov. 29, 1873, in which he cites a line from Daniel in 1595, 'Railing *rhymes* were sowed,' as the earliest instance of the false mode of spelling. If this be so, the case is complete in favour of *rime* (or *ryme*), and no one ought to hesitate about writing the word in one or other of these two ways. Another argument against the derivation from ῥυθμός is the parallel case of the Italian *rima*, which, like *rime*, meant poetry in general. Cf. Ariosto, *Orl. Fur.* I. ii., 'cosa non detta in prosa mai ne in *rima*,' whence Milton took his line *P. L.* i. 16. This, Diez truly observes, could never have come from ῥυθμός, though he is wrong when he goes on to say that the Italian equivalent *must* be 'rimmo' or 'remmo,' because, as a matter of fact, it happens to be 'ritmo.' But when H. Wedgwood (*Dict. Etym.* s. v. **Rhyme**) objects to the former assertion of Diez on account of the analogy of the French *rime* from the older form *rithme*, he seems to overlook an important difference between the two languages in their respective methods of derivation from the Latin. When the original word has two consonants coming together in successive syllables, the Italian either retains the first (changing aspirates to mutes), as in *ritmo, atmosfera*, &c., or else assimilates it to the second, as in *ammirare* from *admirare*, &c.; while in modern French the former consonant usually disappears with compensation, as in *route, soumis, avocat* (true French *avoué*), from *rupta, submissus, advocatus*. Hence *rhythmus* would naturally pass through *rithme* into *rime*, whereas in Italian it could only produce *ritmo* (or else *rimmo* or *remmo*), but not *rimo*, still less *rima*. There is, however, no reason for doubting that both *rima* and the French *rime* are cognate with the Teutonic forms *rim, reim*, &c., above mentioned.

Guerdon (*l.* 73). The received etymology of this word is the O.H.G. *widarlôn*, O.E. *wiðerlean*, which became in Low Latin *widerdonum*, by association with *donum*, 'a gift,' since the word originally meant 'a reward in return for services.' Burguy, in his *Grammaire de la Langue d'Oil*, gives the various forms *gueredon, geredon, werdon*, and *werredon*, also the verbs *guerredoner* and *re-werdoner*; and quotes a sentence from the Sermons of S. Bernard, 'Li granz *rewerdoneres* est venuz,' i.e. 'Le grand *rémunérateur* est venu.' Another derivation, at first sight very plausible, is given by Ménage, who refers the origin of the word to the Old German *Werdung*, which took the form *Werdunia* in Low Latin, and meant

APPENDIX I.

pretii æstimatio. The existence of this latter word is shown by a passage which he quotes from Vossius, *De Vitiis Sermonis Latini* (B. ii. c. 20), where instances occur both of *Werdunia* and of a compound *Cinewerdunia*, which Ducange also gives in his *Glossary*, though *Werdunia* itself is not to be found there. The first part of this compound is of doubtful import and derivation. Chevallet has suggested what is really the same etymology, for he derives *guerdon* from *Werd* (Modern German *Werth*), meaning 'price' or 'value;' but this is rejected by Scheler (*Dict. d'Etymologie Française*, 1863), who pronounces the derivation from *widarlôn* to be 'au-dessus de toute contestation.' It is true that *guerdon* might come from *Werdung* according to the rule by which the letter *w* was regularly replaced by *g* or *gu* in those Teutonic words which the Franks introduced into Gaul (see Max Müller, *Lectures on the Science of Language*, 2nd Series, p. 265); but by the same rule it might equally well be derived from *widarlôn*, and that it was so derived seems to be a well-established historical fact. The really fatal objection to Ménage's theory is the existence of the Italian word *guiderdone*, which could not possibly have had its origin in *Werdung*, though it would naturally be produced from *widarlôn* by the change of *w* into *gu* above mentioned. The older spelling *guerre-don* no doubt arose from the idea that the term had something to do with remuneration for service in *war*.

Felon (*l.* 91). The derivation from *fell*, mentioned in the note, is by no means proved. The word may be connected with the Gaelic *feall*, 'deceit,' for examples of which see H. Wedgwood's *Dict. of Etymology*, s. v. **felon**. Du Cange indeed says that '*felo*' = 'perfidus,' 'rebellis, 'crudelis,' &c., from A.S. *fell*; and Chaucer, in the *Romaunt of the Rose*, takes pains to establish this connexion in the lines—' Daunger that is so *feloun Felly* purposeth thee to werrey, which is full *cruel*, the sooth to say.' Cf. Lyndsay, *Monarchie*, 'that felloun flood;' Pope, *Odyssey*, iv. 712, 'his felon hate.' From this general sense of 'wickedness,' *felony* became a recognised legal term for the higher class of crimes; and since such were formerly punished by the forfeiture of lands and goods, *felon* was erroneously supposed to be a compound of *fee* and *lon*, i.e. the price of a *feof* or beneficiary estate (Spelman in Blackstone's *Commentary*). The Italian *fello* and the French *felle*, 'cruel,' are perhaps traceable to the same root.

Wanton (*l.* 136). Authorities differ as to the origin of this word. H. Wedgwood (*Dict. of Etymology*, s. v.) considers it to be a compound of the O.E. negative prefix *wan* (as in *wan-hope* = 'despair') and *togen*, the past part. of *teon* (G. *ziehen*), 'to draw.' Its meaning would therefore be 'untrained,' and hence 'irregular in conduct.' This derivation is clearly proved by the existence of an intermediate form *wantowen*, of which Wedgwood quotes an instance from a Sermon on Miracle Plays—'We waxen *wantowen* or idil.' He also notes the expressions 'untowen,' 'wel itowen,' 'ful itowen,' in the *Ancren Riwle*, a treatise of the 13th century on the Rules of Monastic Life. (But the meaning of the last word is not, as he gives it, 'fully educated,' but 'undisciplined' or 'ill-educated,' from the O.E. *ful* = 'foul.' See the *Ancren Riwle*, edited by the Rev. J. Morton for the Camden Society, pp. 108, 140, 244, 368.) [An alternative derivation is that given by Webster and others, 'from a Welsh adjective *gwantan*, 'roving,' 'fickle,' which is referred to the verb *gwanta*, 'to separate' (probably cognate with *chwant*, 'lust,' Greek χαίν-ω, Lat. *hi-o*, *hisco*, &c.). The precise similarity both in form and meaning between *gwantan* and *wanton* would no doubt go very far towards establishing a common origin; we cannot, however, certainly say which is the older of the two, and it is more than probable that the Welsh may have borrowed the word from our language. But supposing that *gwantan* was the earlier form, and that from it *wanton* was derived, its resemblance to the real English word *wantowen* might very well give rise to the theory which Wedgwood adopts, especially if at any time after its introduction *wanton* came to be spelt *wantoun* or *wantown*.] All this, however, is purely hypothetical; the history of the word, as traced by Wedgwood, is quite conclusive in favour of the first-named derivation. Notwithstanding, Edward Müller in his *Etymologisches Wörterbuch der englischen Sprache* (1867), accepts the theory propounded by Webster.

Herse (*l.* 151). This word was employed in three distinct senses, of which the last now alone remains in use. These are (1) the *funeral monument* (Spenser, *F. Q.* II. viii. 16); (2) the *coffin*, as in Shaksp. 1 *K. Henry VI.* i. 1, where 'a wooden coffin' is presently spoken of as 'King Henry's *hearse*;' (3) the *funeral carriage*. Richardson, wrongly supposing this last to be the primary meaning, derives the word from the O.E. *hyrstan*, 'to decorate' (see also Horne Tooke's *Diversions of Purley*). It really comes from the French *herce*, Low Latin *hercia* (*hirpicem*), 'a harrow' (Ducange, *Glossary*, s.v.), and originally meant a triangular frame for candles, placed at the head of the corpse. Thus

APPENDIX I.

in the account of the battle of Crecy in Froissart's *Chronicles*, c. 130 (Lord Berners' translation), we are told that 'the archers stode in maner of a *herse*,' i.e. in triangular form. And since this burning of candles was the distinctive feature in the obsequies, the term 'hearse' came to be used either of the whole ceremony or of its various appurtenances (Wedgwood, *Dict. of Etymol.* s. v.). In the *Faery Queen*, III. ii. 48, Spenser has wrongly applied the phrase 'holy herse' to the church service, as if the word were connected with 'rehearse;' and perhaps the same mistake is made in the *Shepheard's Calendar*, xi. 60, where 'herse' is explained in the glossary to mean 'the solemn obsequie in funeralles.'

Trick (*l.* 170). The main senses of this word (as noun and verb) are—(1) Artifice, (2) Peculiar habit or manner (*King Lear*, iv. 6, 'The trick of that voice I do well remember'), (3) Ornament (*Il Penseroso*, 123; Shakspere, *King Henry V.* iii. 6, 'trick up with new-tuned oaths;' *Merry W. of Windsor*, 'trickings for our fairies'), (4) Heraldic devices (Jonson, *Poetaster*, 'they are blazoned, they are tricked'), (5) Collection of cards taken up by the winner. All these find a common origin in the Dutch *trek*, a 'draught,' 'pull,' or 'stroke,' which answers to our word 'draw' in all its senses, and has also the secondary meanings of 'deceit,' and of a 'feature' of the face or character. (Cf. *trait* from *tractus*, which means in French both 'feature' and 'trick.' *Faire des traits = faire des tours*.) To the same root *trek* Diez refers *tricher* (It. *treccare*), 'to cheat,' though he derives *in-triguer*, *trigaud*, &c., from the Latin verb *tricari*. This is unquestionably right, although at first sight *tricher*, with its cognate *triquer*, might seem a natural formation from *tricari*, like *miche* from *mica*, *indiquer* from *indicare*, &c. But, as Diez observes, the radical *e* in the older form *trecher* is fatal to such a derivation, and the Teutonic origin of *tricher* may therefore be considered as established. There cannot be any connexion (however remote) between the Latin *tricari* and the root we have been considering; since we know that the former is derived from *tricæ*, originally Tricæ, a small town in Apulia, whose name with that of the neighbouring Apinæ came to be used of anything trifling or insignificant. (Cf. Pliny, *Nat. Hist.* iii. 16; Martial, *Epigr.* XIV. i. 7, 'Sunt apinæ tricæque et si quid *vilius* istis;' Erasmus, *Chiliad. Cent.* 2, *Adag.* 43, 'Tricas et Apinas vulgo res *futiles et nugatorias* dicebant.') Thus Cicero (*ad Atticum*, x. viii. 9) contrasts 'domesticas tricas' with 'publicam cladem.' Hence *tricari* was applied to shuffling and petty meanness of conduct (Cic. *ad Att.* XIV. xix. 4; XV. iii. 5), a sense which is accidentally almost the same with that of *tricher* and *treccare*. This may be noted as one of those curious coincidences, by which words without any etymological connexion obtain in different languages a similar form and meaning. A further illustration of this is seen in the German *trügen (triegen)*, 'to deceive,' regarded as a collateral form of *tragen*, and thus connected with *traho, draw, drag*, &c. Another meaning of *tricæ* (that of 'perplexity' or 'entanglement') seems to have produced the later Latin *tricare*, 'to loiter;' and this was absurdly derived from *trica* (θρίξ), 'a knot of hair,' for a full account of which see Ducange, *Glossarium*, s. v. trica. This verb also meant 'to deceive,' whence came *tricatores* = 'deceptores, qui res impediunt vel implicant.'

We may therefore assume *trek* to be the original of *trick* in all its senses, as well as of *tricher* and *treccare*; it only remains to reject the derivation given by Dr. Johnson and Richardson of *trick*, in the sense of ornament, from the *trica* above referred to, since the idea of ornament springs most naturally from that of *delineation*, especially when used of heraldic devices (see No. 4 *supra*). The only instance given of the word as actually meaning 'a knot of hair' is from Jonson's *Poetaster*, 'your court curls or your *tricks*;' but this need not be anything more than a general term for 'ornament.' (See the quotation from Sandys' *Travels*, given in the note upon *l.* 170.)

APPENDIX II.

—◆—

On the allusions in ll. 128, 129.

THOSE who have read Professor Masson's examination of this passage in his *Life of Milton* (vol. i. p. 641 foll.) will hardly fail to agree with him in interpreting the 'grim wolf' to mean that system of perversion to Romanism, which seems to have reached its height in or about the year 1637. The view partially adopted by Newton, that the Primate is the person here intended, might seem at first sight to be supported by an entry in Laud's diary, to the effect that in July 1637 a libel was pasted on the Cross at Cheapside, designating him 'the arch-wolf of Canterbury.' But so common an expression as this is barely sufficient of itself to enable us to draw a positive conclusion, while the language which Milton here employs respecting the 'wolf' presents at least a twofold objection to such an interpretation. First, the evil is clearly an *external* one, being distinguished from the abuses previously mentioned as existing *within* the fold—the word 'besides' indicates this—and secondly, the expression 'privy paw,' denoting secresy, would be a most unfit one, if it were intended to describe the doings of Laud and the High Commission Court, whose attacks on Nonconformity were open and undisguised; nor was there perhaps any character more prominent at this time than that of the Archbishop. Both the required conditions are satisfied, if we adopt Newton's alternative explanation, 'besides what the Popish priests privately pervert to their religion,' in support of which view Masson in his *Life of Milton* brings forward the instances of Sir Toby Matthews, Sir Kenelm Digby and others, who had been most active in this matter for some years before the publication of *Lycidas*. He goes on to show that Laud himself strongly disapproved of these perversions, as appears from his letter of remonstrance to Sir K. Digby (March 27, 1636) upon his change of religion, and from his

H

strict injunctions to Dr. Bayly, Vice-chancellor of Oxford (Aug. 29, 1637), to take strong measures against the Jesuits, who were seducing the students in that University. It may have been the case that 'as he valued his theory of a possible union of the churches, the floating off of atoms vexed and annoyed him' (Masson *l. c.*); but even the fact that he did desire such a union is mainly supported by the assertion of Montague, Bp. of Chichester, to Panzani, a Papal agent sent to decide certain disputes among the English Catholics, but with special instructions not to have any dealings whatever with Laud (Lingard, *Hist. of England*, vol. vii. c. 5). Taken in connexion with this injunction, the circumstances attending the offer of a cardinal's hat made to Laud a short time before, and rejected by him on the ground of dissatisfaction with Rome 'as it then was' (*Diary*, Aug. 4, 1633), serve to show that the distrust between the two parties was at least mutual; for it is certain that this offer was made without cognisance of the Pope, who even refused to ratify it when the request to do so was laid before him. We know also that the news of Laud's death in 1646 was hailed at Rome with great rejoicing, on the ground that 'the greatest enemy of the Church of Rome in England was cut off, and the greatest champion of the Church of England silenced.' (Testimony of Sir Lionel Tolmache, as reported by the Rev. J. Whiston, his chaplain about 1666). All this agrees very well with Laud's own assertions in answer to the charges brought against him by the Puritans in 1640, 'that he hath traytorously endeavoured to reconcile the Church of England with the Church of Rome, and permitted a Popish hierarchy in this kingdom, &c.' To this he replies, 'I did never desire that England and Rome should meet, but with the forsaking of error and superstition, if some tenets of Rome on one side and some deep disaffections on the other have not made this impossible, *as I much doubt they have.* But that I should practise with Rome *as it now stands* is utterly untrue. Secondly, I have hindered as many from going to the Roman party, as any divine in England hath done. (Twenty-two names are here quoted, many of whom are of high rank and quality.) Thirdly, many Recusants think that *I have done them and their cause more harm than they which have seemed more fierce against them.*' The obvious fact is that the vital differences between the religious theory of Laud and that of the Roman Church, patent to either party and too great to allow the possibility of a union, were ignored by the Puritans in their zeal against the Laudian movement, which they either did not care to distinguish from actual Popery, or considered as even something worse. (See speech of Lord Falkland, Feb. 9, 1641.) Nor is it likely that Milton, young as he was at this time, surrounded by Puritan influences, and having a strong natural bias in the same direction, would be enabled to form a juster estimate of the facts than the rest of his party did; it is therefore quite likely that he may have wished to include Laud among even the foremost of the Romanisers in the Church of England, though we deny that the allusion in the present passage is directly or exclusively intended for him.

The expression 'nothing said' (altered from 'little said' of the first draft) is plainly an imputation upon the Court and hierarchy for their remissness in dealing with the evil we have just been considering. As regards the latter, if we take Laud as its representative, it is probable (to quote again from Professor Masson) that 'the Puritans, not knowing his measures [against the Catholic agents], or not thinking them enough, found in the increasing number of perversions a fresh condemnation of him and his adherents.' But the policy of Charles I. towards the Papists was by no means uniform. His treaty of marriage with the Princess Henrietta in 1624 had contained a promise of immunity to the Catholics for the peaceable exercise of their worship, though he had sworn in conjunction with his father a few months before, that in case of his marriage with a Catholic the said immunity should extend only to herself and her own family. In 1629 he adopted a middle course, exempting them from the extreme penalties of recusancy in respect of fines for non-attendance at the services of the established Church, yet not allowing them absolute freedom in their own religious worship; and even this concession was loudly reprobated by the Puritans. At the present time (1637) the queen's private influence was considerable. By the strenuous efforts of Con, the successor of Panzani, she had been induced to take a warm interest in the work of individual proselytism, which had superseded the former scheme of reunion of the Churches, and the autumn of this year was marked by a large accession of perverts to Rome. On the whole therefore we may conclude that Milton's words *little* (or *nothing*) *said* are a rather moderate statement of the real grievance, and one with which the Puritans generally would by no means have contented themselves.

Warton is surprised that the University should have allowed these lines, and that they should have escaped 'the severest animadversions' from the High Court of Commission and the Star Chamber. But there had long been a decided Puritan element at Cambridge, the leading man at the time of Charles' accession being Dr. Preston, Master of Emanuel, 'the greatest pupil-monger in England' according to Fuller, formerly a favourite with the Duke of Buckingham, and one of the king's chaplains (Masson, vol. i. p. 94). As to the civil and spiritual tribunals, perhaps Milton was then too obscure to demand their notice; we know at least that he afterwards managed to escape the fate which befell others of his party, and that even after the Restoration in 1660 he was included in the Act of Indemnity, and was released after three days' imprisonment, although his *Eiconoclastes* and *Defensio Populi Anglicani* were ordered to be burnt.

TRANSLATION OF LYCIDAS INTO LATIN HEXAMETERS,

By William Hogg, 1694.

Paraphrasis Latina in duo Poemata (quorum alterum a Miltono, alterum a Clievlando Anglice scriptum fuit) quibus deploratur Mors juvenis præclari et eruditi, D. Edvardi King, qui Nave, quâ vectabatur, Saxo illisa in Oceano Hybernico submersus est.

Authore Gulielmo Hogæo.

Author lamentatur amicum eruditum, infeliciter Mari Hyberno submersum, postquam a Cestria solvisset, 1637. Et, occasione oblata, corruptorum Clericorum ruinam prædicit, qui tunc temporis pro libitu in sublimi dignitatis gradu vitam agitabant :—

 Rursus odoratæ myrti laurique virentes,
 Vestitæ aureolos hedera serpente corymbos,
 Rursus ego vestras redeo decerpere baccas,
 Quanquam acidas, nec dum maturo sole recoctas ;
 Et vestras spoliare comas et spargere passim,   5
 Frigora quanquam absunt procul autumnalia, nec dum
 Hispidus arboreos Aquilo populatur honores.
 Me dolor, et duri necopina injuria fati
 Tempora vestra meis cogunt turbare querelis.
 Occidit heu ! teneræ Lycidas in flore juventæ,   10
 Occidit heu ! dulcis Lycidas, nullumque reliquit
 Ille parem. Blandi Lycidæ jam funera justis
 Deplorare modis quis non velit ? Ipse canendi
 Arte Sophocleum didicit transire cothurnum.
 Arva per æquorei infletum fluitare profundi   15
 Tene decet ? nullis digna an tua fata querelis,
 Dum te fluctus habet, versantque per æquora venti ?
 Nunc utinam eloquii charites, et vivida vocum

Gratia, quas olim est veterum turba impia vatum
Aonias mentita deas, mihi protinus adsint, 20
Jucundaque novam modulentur arundine musam.
Forsitan et nostras pariter comitabitur umbras
Carmine Musa pio, cinerique precabitur hospes
Præteriens, 'Tacita placidus requiesce sub urna.'
Unicus amborum pariter juvenilibus annis 25
Mons nutritor erat, pariter quoque pavimus unum
Ambo gregem gelidos jucundi fontis ad ortus,
Aut rivi salientis aquas, aut arboris umbram.
Ambo simul teneras ad pascua læta capellas
Duximus, ante oculis quam pulchra Aurora reclusis 30
Reddiderat lucemque orbi rebusque colorem.
Et simul exiguæ jucundo murmure muscæ
Noctivagam resonare tubam exaudivimus ambo
Per placidos Lunæ cursus, jam rore recenti
Nectareos spargente gregis per vellera succos. 35
Sæpe etiam haud seræ libuit decedere nocti,
Donec ab Eoa nitido quæ vespere lympha
Stella exorta fuit medii transivit Olympi
Culmen, et Hesperias cursum convertit ad undas.
Interea, harmonicas digitis moderantibus auras, 40
Agrestem inflamus calamum, choreasque pilosi
In numerum ducunt Satyri, Faunique nequibant
Capripedes nostris cohibere a cantibus aurem ;
Ipse senex nostra Damœtas gestit avena.
 Heu male mutatæ Fortunæ injuria ! vadis, 45
Vadis ad æternas (nunquam heu ! rediture) tenebras.
Te, Pastor, silvæ umbriferæ, viridesque recessus
Antrorum, quot ubique thymo vel vite teguntur,
Undique jure dolent, resonatque dolentibus Echo.
Ah ! salices cessant virides humilesque myricæ 50
Nunc resonare tuæ ramosque inflectere Musæ.
Ut nocet atra rosis ærugo, ut pestis acerba est
Œstrum immane boum, glacialia frigora flores
Qualiter infestant tunica variante decoros,
Cum niveus primum florescere cœpit acanthus ; 55
Sic quoque pastores (triste ac miserabile !) lethi,
O Lycida dilecte, tui dolor urit acerbus.
 Quæ nemora, aut qui vos saltus habuere, puellæ
Naiades, immensis Lycidas cum est obrutus undis ?

Nam neque duxistis choreas super ardua rupis 60
Culmina præruptæ, Druidum monumenta priorum ;
Nec vos saxosæ tenuere cacumina Monæ,
Nec Deva fatidicas ubi late exporrigit undas.
Cur ego vana loquor ? præsens si vestra fuisset
Tota cohors, huic ecquid opem auxiliumque tulisset ? 65
Orphei Calliopea suo quam ferre valebat
Tristis opem ? nil Musa suo succurrere nato,
Cujus ad interitum rerum natura dolebat,
Tunc potuit, cum femineæ furor iraque turbæ,
Discerptum latos juvenem quæ sparsit in agros, 70
Sanguineum caput Orpheia cervice revulsum,
Hebre, tuis injecit aquis, quod adusque cucurrit
Littora, quæ miseri letho bene nota Leandri.
 Quid juvat assiduis frustra tabescere curis,
Et pastoralis studium contemnere vitæ, 75
Et vanum ingratæ Musæ impendisse laborem ?
Nonne fuit satius sociorum more per umbras
Suaviter arboreas sectari Amaryllida dulcem,
Atque, Neæra, tuos leviter prensare capillos.
Fama viros, quorum sublimi in pectore virtus 80
Se generosa locat, cohibere libidinis æstum
(Pessima nobilium solet esse hæc lerna virorum)
Incitat, et duros etiam sufferre labores.
Ast ubi pæne tibi illustris tetigisse videris
Culmen honoris, adest Lachesis cum forcipe dira, 85
Et fragilis vitæ filum secat. At mihi Phœbus
'Fama tamen post fata manet, secura sepulchri'
Dixerat, et tremulas leviter mihi vellicat aures ;
'Fama est planta solo minime prognata caduco ;
'Fortunæ secura nitet, nec fascibus ullis 90
'Erigitur, plausuve petit clarescere vulgi.
'Judicis ante Jovæ purissima lumina lucem
'Illa cupit fulgere suam ; quicunque verendum
'Illius ante thronum laudemque decusque reportat,
'Hujus in æthereo fama effulgebit Olympo.' 95
 O Arethusa, et tu, fluvius celeberrime, Minci,
Undique vocali redimitus arundine frontem,
Lene fluens, quæ nunc recito mihi dicta fuerunt
Hæc longe graviore sono, graviore cothurno ;
Sed mea propositam repetat nunc fistula Musam. 100

Tunc quoque cæruleus vada per Neptunia Triton
Circumagebat iter liquidum, fluctusque sonoros,
Perfidaque Æolios interrogat agmina ventos,
' Unde hæc sæva bono pecoris data fata magistro?'
Quæcunque altisonis ullo de monte procellis   105
Horrida flabra volant, ruptæve cacumine rupis,
Ille rogat; miseri cuncta hæc tamen inscia fati.
Hippotadesque sagax cunctorum nomine tales
Reddidit ore sonos,—' Nullius flamina venti
Nuper ab Æoliis sese effudere cavernis.'   110
Ridebant taciti tranquilla silentia ponti,
Et placido lapsu Panope centumque sorores
Æquora plana legunt stratamque æqualiter undam.
Perfida navis erat, crudeli dedita fato,
Quæ rimis accepit aquam, sacrumque repente   115
Mersit in ima caput, medioque sub æquore texit.

    Proximus incessu senior tardissimus ibat
Camus, et hirsuta velatus veste; galerus
Carice factus erat, variis obscura figuris
Quem textura notat, quem circum vitta colori   120
Par, Hyacinthe, tuo, questus inscripte, cucurrit.
' Heu! mihi quis rapuit carissima pignora?' dixit.
Ultimus huc venit, rediitque hinc ultimus, undæ
Cui Galilæanæ custodia creditur; illi
Duplex clavis erat duplici formata metallo,   125
(Aurea portam aperit, subito quam ferrea claudit).
Tempora tum nitida quassans ornata tiara
Talia fatus erat tetricæ cum murmure vocis.
' Quam bene nunc pro te, si vertere fata liceret,
' Quam bene nunc pro te, juvenum carissime, multos   130
' Concessissem alios, stimulante cupidine ventris
' Qui furtim ac tacite irrumpunt et ovilia scandunt!
' Unica cura quibus pecorum fuit usque magistri
' Vi rapuisse epulas, avidique hausisse paratas,
' Convivasque alios audaci pellere dextra.   135
' O cæci ventres, qui vix comprendere dextra
' Pastorale pedum, aut aliquid didicere, fideles
' Quod juvat atque decet pecorum præstare magistros!
' Quid curant? quid curæ opus est? bene vivitur illis;
' Et licet his, ubicunque libet, sub vindice nullo   140

LYCIDAS.

'Stridenti miserum stipula disperdere carmen.
'Interea pecudes languentia lumina volvunt,
'Tabescuntque fame, miseris quia pabula desunt;
'Sed ventis nebulisque tument, sensimque putrescunt
'Interius, sparguntque sui contagia morbi. 145
'Insuper et teneras vis quotidiana luporum
'Clam discerpit oves avidamque immergit in alvum.
'Machina sed gemino ad portas armata flagello
'Protinus his uno parat ictu accersere fatum.'
 Nunc, Alphee, tuos iterum convertere cursus 150
Incipe! nunc vox dira abiit, vox dira quievit,
Quæ fluvium terrore tuum retro ire coegit.
Tu quoque, pastoris Siculi modulamine quondam
Edita Musa, redi, nemorumque umbracla colores
Huc florum innumeros simul injectare jubeto. 155
Vos quoque nunc valles humiles, ubi florea Tempe
Et venti placidis resonant fluviique susurris,
Quarum haud sæpe sinus Cancri ferus attigit ardor.
Undique gemmantes oculos conferte, virenti
Nectareos quicunque bibunt in cespite succos; 160
Floribus et vernis totam depingite terram.
Huc rosa, jucundi quæ dicta est primula veris,
Quæ moritur, si spreta jacet, pulcherque hyacinthus;
Huc quoque cum niveis vaccinia nigra ligustris,
Huc quoque sylvarum cum garyophillide cana 165
Moschitæque rosæ violarum et amabile germen,
Atque periclymenos fulgenti ornatus amictu;
Paralysisque etiam, fulvo quæ tota metallo
Pallet, et in terram pendente cacumine vergit,
Et quicunque gerit tunicam flos luctibus aptam, 170
Conveniant, pariterque locum glomerentur in unum.
Huc, Amaranthe, veni, quem non borealia lædunt
Frigora, quem æstiferi non torrent brachia Cancri!
Huc, Narcisse, veni, lacrimis tua pocula replens
Suavibus! huc flores veniant, quoscunque vocavi, 175
Laurigerique tegant Lycidæ venerabile bustum.
Gaudia sic mœstis juvat interponere curis,
Solarique animos ficta sub imagine nostros;
Dum te fluctus agit, ventisque sonantia volvunt
Æquora vasta, trahuntque tuum retrahuntque cadaver. 180

Sive ultra æstiferis ferventes Hebridas undis,
(Hic tu forte lates rapido sub gurgite tectus,
Imaque monstriferi visis penetralia mundi,)
Sive remotus abes procul hinc, longumque soporem
Carpis, ubi sedem tenuit Bellerus avitam,   185
Pristina quem veterum celebrant mendacia vatum,
Mons ubi præsidio circumdatus undique spectat
Namancon, spectatque tuos, Bayona, recessus;—
Ad patrias sedes precor o precor, Angele, rursus
Respice nunc miseros non aversatus amicos!   190
Vos quoque, delphines, juveni supponite tergum,
Perque plagas vasti vitreas portate profundi!
    Nunc pecorum placidi fletus inhibete magistri.
Non periit letho Lycidas cessitve sepulchri
Legibus, æquorea jaceat licet obrutus unda.   195
Haud aliter Phœbi se prævia stella profundum
Mergit in Hesperium, diversis rursus ab undis
Mane novo surgens, multo spectabilis auro,
Erigit illa caput primoque ardescit Eoo.
Sic Lycidas primum ima petit, dein ardua scandit,   200
Præside nempe illo, tumidi qui terga profundi
Haud secus ac siccam pedibus peragravit arenam,
Spumeaque intrepidis calcavit marmora plantis.
Hic alios inter silvæ nemoralis honores,
Atque alios longe fluvios se nectare puro   205
Obruit, atque suos miro lavit amne capillos,
Ætheriosque hilari lætus trahit aure hymenæos
In regnis ubi floret amor et pura voluptas.
Hic quoque Sanctorum chorus illum amplectitur omnis,
Ordine qui juncti pariter cœlestia cantant   210
Carmina et ætherias ducunt cantando choreas,
Atque oculis abigunt lacrymam procul illius omnem.
Nunc pecorum placidi Lycidam lugere magistri
Absistunt; tu, littoreas dum carpis arenas,
(Hæc tibi in Elysiis durabunt præmia campis)   215
Semper eris quovis meliorque et faustior astro
Puppe periclosam trepida tranantibus undam.
    Talia concinuit peregrinus carmina pastor
Quercubus alticomis fluviorum et lenibus undis,
Dum croceis Aurora rotis invecta redibat;   220

LYCIDAS.

Mutabatque sonos relegens, orisque recursu
Dissimili tenuem variabat arundine ventum.
Jam sol majores umbras super alta tetendit
Culmina et Hesperiis post paulo absconditur undis.
Tandem iterum rediit viridemque remisit amictum ;   225
'Cras sylvas peragrare novas, nova pascua, cordi est.'

NOTES.

In *l.* 75 the English has *end* misprinted for *tend*.
l. 92 Qy. *Jovis?* but *Jovæ* is clearly printed.
l. 96 Qy. *fluviûm* (for *fluviorum*)?
l. 213, *Now Lycidas the shepherds weep no more* in the English.

EPITAPHIUM DAMONIS.

Argumentum.

THYRSIS et DAMON, ejusdem viciniæ pastores, eadem studia sequuti, a pueritia amici erant, ut qui plurimum. Thyrsis animi causa profectus peregre de obitu Damonis nuncium accepit. Demum postea reversus, et rem ita esse comperto, se suamque solitudinem hoc carmine deplorat. Damonis autem sub persona hic intelligitur *Carolus Deodatus* ex urbe Hetruriæ Luca paterno genere oriundus, cætera Anglus; ingenio, doctrina, clarissimisque cæteris virtutibus, dum viveret, juvenis egregius.

HIMERIDES nymphæ (nam vos et Daphnin et Hylan,
Et plorata diu meministis fata Bionis),
Dicite Sicelicum Thamesina per oppida carmen :
Quas miser effudit voces, quæ murmura Thyrsis,
Et quibus assiduis exercuit antra querelis,   5
Fluminaque, fontesque vagos, nemorumque recessus ;

1 **Himerides**] of Himera in Sicily. Symmons, in his *Life of Milton* (appended to the *Prose Works*), aptly observes that Warton should not call it 'the famous bucolic river of Theocritus,' since none of his scenes are laid there, and the river is only mentioned twice in the *Idylls* (v. 124 ; vii. 74).

Hylan] The first syllable is short, as appears from Theocr. *Id.* vii. ; Virg. *E.* vi. 43, *G.* iii. 6. Milton himself has 'raptus Hӯlas' in *Eleg.* vii. 24. Possibly he may have been thinking of Hȳlæus in Virg. *G.* ii. 457. Daphnis, Hylas, and Bion are lamented in Theocr. i. 13, and Moschus, *Id.* iii., respectively.

3] Virg. *G.* ii. 176, 'Ascræumque cano Romana per oppida carmen.' 'Thamesina' fixes the locality to Horton and its neighbourhood, where the Colne (*l.* 149) joins the Thames.

4 **Thyrsis**] (who of course represents Milton himself) is also the name of the attendant Spirit in *Comus*. It is adopted from Theocr. *Id.* i. (*l. c.*).

5 **exercuit antra**] something like 'exercere diem' in Virg. *Æn.* x. 808. The notion is that of keeping the caves hard at work in echoing his lamentations. Cf. *l.* 8 and note.

6 **fluminaquē fontesque**] an obvious imitation of Virg. *Æn.* iii. 91, 'liminaquē laurusque dei.' It is doubtful whether this instance justifies the licence of the present line, Virgil's practice being confined to those cases in which the next word

EPITAPHIUM DAMONIS.

Dum sibi præreptum queritur Damona, neque altam
Luctibus exemit noctem, loca sola pererrans.
Et jam bis viridi surgebat culmus arista,
Et totidem flavas numerabant horrea messes, 10
Ex quo summa dies tulerat Damona sub umbras,
Nec dum aderat Thyrsis; pastorem scilicet illum
Dulcis amor Musæ Tusca retinebat in urbe :
Ast ubi mens expleta domum, pecorisque relicti
Cura vocat, simul assueta seditque sub ulmo, 15
Tum vero amissum tum denique sentit amicum,
Cœpit et immensum sic exonerare dolorem.

begins with a liquid (as above), a double consonant, as 'Euriquē Zephyrique,' *G.* i. 371, or with the letter *s*, as 'Chloreaquē Syharimque,' *Æn.* xii. 363. Mr. Nettleship, in his *Excursus* at the end of the third volume of Conington's *Virgil*, points out that in this respect Virgil has strictly followed Homer.

8 exemit] 'released' from the task of repeating his lament. Prof. Masson well translates the passage, 'compelling even the midnight Into the sound of his woe.' 'Luctibus' is probably the ablative, that being the usual construction in the Augustan age; but the dative is used by later writers. Cf. Tac. *Ann.* xiv. 48, 'ut morti eximeretur.'

9 bis] i.e. in 1638 and 1639. The *Epitaphium Damonis* was written towards the end of the latter year, and Diodati seems to have died in the summer of 1638 (Masson, *Life of Milton*, vol. i. p. 776).

13 Dulcis amor Musæ] See in the *Argument* the words '*animi causa* profectus peregre.' Milton here refers to his second visit to Florence in the beginning of 1639, which lasted two months. Of the first he thus speaks in the *Defensio Secunda pro populo Anglicano*: 'Illic multorum et nobilium sane et doctorum hominum familiaritatem statim contraxi, quorum privatas academias assidue frequentavi.' Among these friends were Carlo Dati and Francini (*l.* 137), the former of whom addressed to him the Latin letter inscribed 'Joanni Miltoni Londiniensi, &c.'; the latter the complimentary Italian ode beginning 'Ergimi all' etra o Clio.' The 'private academies' were literary societies for the mutual acquaintance and friendship of learned men, for admission to which each member had to give some 'proof of his talent or learning,' as Milton tells us in the *Reason of Church Government*. He probably there recited some of his early Latin poems, which won for him the encomiums above referred to (Masson, vol. i. pp. 719 foll.).

15 assueta sub ulmo] i.e. at his father's house at Horton; possibly the 'dilectas villarum ulmos' mentioned in the seventh of the *Prolusiones Oratoriæ*, delivered at Cambridge. Elms still form a prominent feature in the scenery about Horton. Warton compares the 'accustomed oak,' *Il Penseroso*, 60. For the postposition of -*que*, cf. Propert. II. xvi. 11, 'ferratam Danaes transiliam*que* domum;' Tibull. I. iii. 55, 'Messalam terra dum sequitur*que* mari.'

EPITAPHIUM DAMONIS.

Ite domum impasti, domino jam non vacat, agni.
Hei mihi! quæ terris, quæ dicam numina cœlo,
Postquam te immiti rapuerunt funere, Damon!   20
Siccine nos linquis, tua sic sine nomine virtus
Ibit, et obscuris numero sociabitur umbris?
At non ille, animas virga qui dividit aurea,
Ista velit, dignumque tui te ducat in agmen,
Ignavumque procul pecus arceat omne silentum.   25
    Ite domum impasti, domino jam non vacat, agni.
Quicquid erit, certe nisi me lupus ante videbit,
Indeplorato non comminuere sepulchro,
Constabitque tuus tibi honos, longumque vigebit
Inter pastores : Illi tibi vota secundo   30
Solvere post Daphnin, post Daphnin dicere laudes,
Gaudebunt, dum rura Pales, dum Faunus amabit :
Si quid id est, priscamque fidem coluisse piumque,
Palladiasque artes, sociumque habuisse canorum.
    Ite domum impasti, domino jam non vacat, agni.   35
Hæc tibi certa manent, tibi erunt hæc præmia, Damon;
At mihi quid tandem fiet modo? quis mihi fidus

23] Hor. *Od.* I. xxiv. 15 : 'Non vanæ redeat sanguis imagini, Quam virga semel horrida . . . Nigro compulerit Mercurius *gregi*' (*l.* 25). For 'aurea' cf. Hom. *Od.* x. 277, where Hermes is called χρυσόρραπις. Lucian has the same simile, αὐτὸς . . . ὥσπερ τι αἰπόλιον ἀθρόους αὐτοὺς τῇ ῥάβδῳ σοβῶν.

25 **silentum**] used absolutely of the dead in Virg. *Æn.* vi. 432. The 'ignavum pecus' is from *G.* iv. 168, where it has quite a different application. Keightley notes the expression 'pecus' as 'strange,' but its use here is justified by 'gregi' in the passage from Horace quoted above.

27 **nisi me, &c.**] i.e. ' if I do not lose my power of utterance.' See Virg. *E.* ix. 54 for the superstition that if a wolf saw a man first, the latter became dumb.

28] Cf. *Lycidas,* 14. Warton quotes Ovid, *Trist.* III. iii. 45.

31] Cf. Virg. *E.* v. 78-80, where Daphnis, the great pastoral hero, is promised divine honours equal, to those paid to Bacchus and Ceres.

33 **priscamque fidem, &c.**] 'the faith of the old and the loyal' (Masson), i.e. the good old-fashioned rustic faith. Keightley questions the correctness of this use of 'pium' as a substantive. It certainly sounds somewhat harsh in connexion with 'fidem,' but the expression itself may be paralleled by the 'honestum,' 'utile,' &c., so common in Cicero's philosophical treatises, which are imitations of the Greek τὸ καλόν, &c.

37 **modo**] probably an adverb of time = 'now.' It is more commonly

EPITAPHIUM DAMONIS.

Hærebit lateri comes, ut tu sæpe solebas
Frigoribus duris et per loca feta pruinis,
Aut rapido sub sole, siti morientibus herbis? 40
Sive opus in magnos fuit eminus ire leones,
Aut avidos terrere lupos præsepibus altis;
Quis fando sopire diem, cantuque, solebit?
    Ite domum impasti, domino jam non vacat, agni.
Pectora cui credam? quis me lenire docebit 45
Mordaces curas, quis longam fallere noctem
Dulcibus alloquiis, grato cum sibilat igni
Molle pyrum et nucibus strepitat focus, et malus Auster
Miscet cuncta foris et desuper intonat ulmo?
    Ite domum impasti, domino jam non vacat, agni. 50
Aut æstate, dies medio dum vertitur axe,
Cum Pan æsculea somnum capit abditus umbra,
Et repetunt sub aquis sibi nota sedilia nymphæ,
Pastoresque latent, stertit sub sepe colonus;
Quis mihi blanditiasque tuas, quis tum mihi risus 55
Cecropiosque sales referet cultosque lepores?
    Ite domum impasti, domino jam non vacat, agni.
  At jam solus agros, jam pascua solus oberro,
Sicubi ramosæ densantur vallibus umbræ;

employed with past tenses than with the future.

39 **feta pruinis**] Virg. *Æn.* i. 51, 'loca *feta* furentibus Austris.'

43 **sopire diem**] like 'condere soles,' Virg. *E.* ix. 52.

46] Todd comp. 'eating cares,' *L'Allegro*, 135, and 'curis mordacibus,' Lucan, *Phars.* ii. 681.

48 **nucibus**] probably 'chestnuts,' sc. 'castaneis.' Cf. Virg. *E.* ii. 52.

49 **miscet cuncta**] 'blurs all the landscape.' (See also Masson's Translation.) Cf. Virg. *G.* i. 359, *Æn.* iv. 160.

51] Lucan. *Phars.* iii. 423, 'medio cum Phœbus in axe est.'

There is a slight confusion between the notion of midday and that of the earth's turning on its axis; 'medio' implying that the revolution is half completed.

52] From Theocr. *Id.* i. 16, where the goatherd refuses to accept Thyrsis' invitation to sing, for fear of disturbing Pan during his midday *siesta*.

53] A partial reminiscence of Virg. *Æn.* i. 167. 'Sibi' is probably to be taken after 'nota,' but is not wanted in the sentence.

56 **Cecropios**] = *Atticos.* Virg. *G.* iv. 177. For 'Attic salt' cf. Mart. *Epigr.* III. xx. 9, 'lepore tinctos Atticos sales.'

Hic serum expecto ; supra caput imber et Eurus   60
Triste sonant, fractæque agitata crepuscula silvæ.
  Ite domum impasti, domino jam non vacat, agni.
Heu, quam culta mihi prius arva procacibus herbis
Involvuntur, et ipsa situ seges alta fatiscit !
Innuba neglecto marcescit et uva racemo,   65
Nec myrteta juvant ; ovium quoque tædet, at illæ
Mœrent, inque suum convertunt ora magistrum.
  Ite domum impasti, domino jam non vacat, agni.
Tityrus ad corylos vocat, Alphesibœus ad ornos,
Ad salices Aegon, ad flumina pulcher Amyntas ;   70
'Hic gelidi fontes, hic illita gramina musco,

60 **serum**] Livy, vii. 8, 'serum erat *diei*.' Neither Ovid nor Virgil appears to have used the word as a noun in this sense.

61 **agitata crepuscula silvæ**] = *silva per crepusculum agitata*. Keightley explains it of 'the twilight or doubtful light caused by the foliage,' and refers to the 'shadows hrown' of *Il Penseroso*, 134, and the 'chequered shade' of *L'Allegro*, 96. Symmons quotes also from Cowper, *Task*, B. i. 347—

    'so sportive is the light,
Shot through the boughs, it dances
    as they dance,
Shadow and sunshine intermingling
    quick.'

64] Keightley well observes that the land 'cracks *æstu* not *situ* (Virg. *G.* i. 72),' but he is wrong in supposing that 'seges' cannot mean the ground itself, since it is distinctly used in this sense by Virgil in *G.* i. 47 and iv. 129. In the former passage 'seges' is the land after ploughing, but before any seed is sown, and in the latter it is the soil with reference to its future produce. Here however the addition of 'alta' (which must mean *tall*) seems to force us to translate 'seges' 'a field of standing corn,' which will not make any sense with 'fatiscit.' Masson's translation, 'the tall corn *sickens* with mildew,' does not accurately render the Latin verb.

65] For the 'marriage' of the vine with larger trees, see the passages cited on *Lycidas*, 40; also *P. L.* v. 215 foll. 'Uva' here must be the vine itself, as in Virg. *G.* ii. 60, 'fert uva racemos.' It is difficult to see the force of Keightley's objection to its being 'joined with "racemo," which is a part of it.' The latter is of course a modal ablative, or else the ablative absolute.

67] Referred to on *Lycidas*, 125.

69] 'Tityrus' &c. are all from Virgil's *Eclogues*. 'Milton may or may not have had particular acquaintances of his in view under these names' (Masson).

71] Partly imitated from Gallus' invitation to Lycoris, Virg. *E.* x. 42; the original is in Theoc. v. 33. 'Illita,' which means 'smeared' or 'spread on the surface,' does not accurately express the idea of moss growing among grass. Perhaps *consita*, or *intersita* (omitting 'hic'), would have been better.

EPITAPHIUM DAMONIS.

'Hic Zephyri, hic placidas interstrepit arbutus undas:'
Ista canunt surdo, frutices ego nactus abibam.
   Ite domum impasti, domino jam non vacat, agni.
Mopsus ad haec—nam me redeuntem forte notarat— 75
(Et callebat avium linguas, et sidera Mopsus,)
'Thyrsi, quid hoc?' dixit, 'quae te coquit improba bilis?
'Aut te perdit amor, aut te male fascinat astrum;
'Saturni grave saepe fuit pastoribus astrum,
'Intimaque obliquo figit praecordia plumbo.' 80
   'Ite domum impasti, domino jam non vacat, agni.
Mirantur nymphae, et 'Quid te, Thyrsi, futurum est?

73] 'Surdo canere' was a proverb. Cf. Virg. *E.* x. 8, 'non canimus surdis;' Propert. IV. viii. 47, 'cantabunt surdo.' Langhorne ludicrously misunderstands the latter part of this line, when he translates it '*I cut my shrubs* (!) and careless walked away.'

76] So in Virg. *Æn.* iii. 360, Æneas addresses Helenus, 'qui sidera sentis, Et volucrum linguas et praepetis omina pennae;' and in x. 176 Asilas is named as the seer 'cui sidera parent Et linguae volucrum.' Keightley is probably right in observing that 'ávium' should be long by position, as 'āriete' &c. in Virgil. As an instance most closely resembling the one in the text, cf. Virg. *G.* i. 482, 'flūviorum rex Eridanus.'

77] For 'coquere,' denoting mental disturbance, cf. Virg. *Æn.* vii. 345, 'curaeque iraeque coquebant;' also Silius Italicus, xiv. 103, 'quos ira metusque coquebat.'

78] For the lengthening of 'amōr' cf. Virg. *E.* x. 69; *Æn.* ii. 369, xi. 323, and other passages. Mr. Nettleship, in his *Excursus* referred to on *l.* 6, ascribes this usage in Virgil to the influence of Ennius, who always makes these endings in -*or* long because of the original Greek -ωρ; but he thinks Virgil was ignorant of this reason, since he never indulges in the license except *in arsi.* Hogg has done the same in his version of *Lycidas*, 208.

fascinat] said of the evil eye in witchcraft, Virg. *E.* iii. 103. For the supposed influence of the stars, see on *Lycidas*, 138.

79] Warton quotes Propert. IV. i. 84, 'et grave Saturni sidus in omne caput,' as showing that this planet was considered to be generally noxious; although there is no apparent reason why shepherds should be specially affected by it. Possibly the Saturnine melancholy and gloom (see opening lines of *Il Penseroso*) may be intended by way of contrast to the joyous ideal of pastoral life.

80 obliquo] partly continues the allusion contained in 'fascinat,' the notion being that of a sidelong envious glance. Cf. 'obliquo oculo,' Hor. *Ep.* I. xiv. 37. 'Plumbo,' because lead was Saturn's metal in alchemy.

82 nymphae et] For the *hiatus* cf. Virg. *E.* iii. 6; *G.* i. 4, 'pecorī et,' &c.

quid te futurum est] There seems to be no authority for this use of the verb 'esse with' the ablative.

'Quid tibi vis?' aiunt; 'non hæc solet esse juventæ
'Nubila frons oculique truces vultusque severi;
'Illa choros lususque leves et semper amorem   85
'Jure petit: bis ille miser qui serus amavit.'
   Ite domum impasti, domino jam non vacat, agni.
Venit Hyas Dryopeque et filia Baucidis Aegle,
Docta modos citharæque sciens, sed perdita fastu;
Venit Idumanii Chloris vicina fluenti;   90
Nil me blanditiæ, nil me solantia verba,
Nil me si quid adest movet, aut spes ulla futuri.
   Ite domum impasti, domino jam non vacat, agni.
Hei mihi! quam similes ludunt per prata juvenci,
Omnes unanimi secum sibi lege sodales!   95
Nec magis hunc alio quisquam secernit amicum
De grege; sic densi veniunt ad pabula thoes,
Inque vicem hirsuti paribus junguntur onagri:
Lex eadem pelagi; deserto in littore Proteus

'Quid me *fiet*' would be an ordinary phrase, as well as 'de me' or 'mihi.'
   83 **nubila frons**] Cf. Hor. *Ep.* I. xviii. 94 'Deme supercilio nubem.'
   86 **bis**] is certainly short, as appears from Ov. *Met.* xiv. 386, 'Tum bis ad Occasum, bis se convertit ad Ortum,' and from its compounds, as 'bĭfidus,' 'bĭmaris,' &c. For the sentiment, Langhorne compares Guarini, *Pastor Fido*, Act i. Sc. 1:
'Che se t' assale a la canuta etate
   Amoroso talento,
Avrai doppio tormento;
E di quel che potendo non volesti,
E di quel che volendo non potrai.'
   88] 'Aegle Naiadum pulcherrima,' Virg. *E.* vi. 20. Keightley suggests that these may have been real ladies of Milton's acquaintance (see on *l.* 69). The particular description which follows makes this very probable. We know however from the lines appended to the 7th Elegy, that the charms of the other sex had no great attractions for Milton. (See note on *Lycidas*, 68, 69.)
   89] From Hor. *Od.* III. ix. 9, 'Dulces docta modos et citharæ sciens.'
   90 **Idumanii fluenti**] the Chelmer, in Essex. Drayton, *Polyolbion*, 19th Song, 95 foll.
   95 **secum sibi**] perhaps an unnecessary pleonasm (as in *l.* 53), but scarcely 'indistinct,' as Keightley objects.
   97 **thoes**] probably 'jackals,' Pliny, *N. H.* viii. 34. θῶες, Hom. *Il.* xiii. 103.
   98 **onagri**] Virg. *G.* iii. 409. Keightley observes that 'the *onager* is not "hirsutus."'
   99]. For the story of Proteus and the sea-calves, see Hom. *Od.* iv. 402 foll.; Virg. *G.* iv. 432 foll.

Agmina ῑ hocarum numerat, vilisque volucrum 100
Passer habet semper quicum sit, et omnia circum
Farra libens volitet, sero sua tecta revisens ;
Quem si sors letho objecit, seu milvus adunco
Fata tulit rostro, seu stravit arundine fossor,
Protinus ille alium socio petit inde volatu. 105
Nos durum genus, et diris exercita fatis
Gens homines, aliena animis et pectore discors,
Vix sibi quisque parem de millibus invenit unum ;
Aut si sors dederit tandem non aspera votis,
Illum inopina dies, qua non speraveris hora, 110
Surripit æternum linquens in sæcula damnum.

    Ite domum impasti, domino jam non vacat, agni.
Heu quis me ignotas traxit vagus error in oras
Ire per aerias rupes Alpemque nivosam !
Ecquid erat tanti Romam vidisse sepultam, 115
(Quamvis illa foret, qualem dum viseret olim,
Tityrus ipse suas et oves et rura reliquit ;)
Ut te tam dulci possem caruisse sodale !

105 **socio**] can properly only apply to the bird when actually mated ; yet this sense would be inconsistent with 'petit,' which describes the *object* of its flight.

106] Cf. Virg. *G.* i. 63, 'homines . . . durum genus.'

exercita fatis] Virg. *Æn.* v. 725, 'Iliacis exercite fatis.' So 'exercita curis,' *ib.* 779.

107] By substituting a comma for the semicolon after 'discors,' the sentence 'nos, &c.' becomes an *anacoluthon*, continued by 'quisque . . . invenit.'

108 **parem unum**] 'one kindred mind' (Cowper),

114] According to Milton's own account of his travels (*Defensio Secunda pro Pop. Angl.*) he did not go into Italy over the Alps, but from Paris into Provence, and thence by ship from Nice to Genoa.

115]) Taken (as Warton remarks) from Virg. *E.* i. 27, 'Et quæ tanta fuit Romam tibi caussa videndi ?' The direct reference to that passage in the next line makes this certain ; otherwise the present line is not so closely imitated from Virgil as to warrant Prof. Masson's assertion that it is 'all but a quotation.' The sense is, 'Was it so well worth my while to visit Rome in ruins, even if it had been now as great as it was in the days of old ?'

116 **dum viseret**] 'in his desire to visit,' lit. 'so long as he might visit ;' *dum = dummodo.* Cf. Virg. *G.* iv. 457, 'dum fugeret ;' *Æn.* i. 5, 'dum conderet urbem.'

118 **sodale**] usually 'sodali,' be

Possem tot maria alta tot interponere montes,
Tot silvas tot saxa tibi fluviosque sonantes! 120
Ah certe extremum licuisset tangere dextram,
Et bene compositos placide morientis ocellos,
Et dixisse, 'Vale, nostri memor ibis ad astra.'

    Ite domum impasti, domino jam non vacat, agni.
Quamquam etiam vestri nunquam meminisse pigebit, 125
Pastores Tusci, Musis operata juventus,
Hic Charis, atque Lepos; et Tuscus tu quoque Damon,
Antiqua genus unde petis Lucumonis ab urbe.
O ego quantus eram, gelidi cum stratus ad Arni
Murmura, populeumque nemus, qua mollior herba, 130
Carpere nunc violas nunc summas carpere myrtos,
Et potui Lycidæ certantem audire Menalcam!

---

cause originally an adjective. The abl. in *e* does however sometimes occur, e.g. Plin. *Epist.* ii. 13, 'sodale jucundius.'

119] Warton compares *Eleg.* iv. 21 (to Diodati)—

'Hei mihi, quot pelagi, quot montes interjecti
  Me faciunt alia parte carere mei;'

on which he refers to Hom. *Il.* i. 156—

ἐπεὶ ἡ μάλα πολλὰ μεταξὺ
οὔρεά τε σκιόεντα θάλασσά τε ἠχήεσσα,

and to Ovid, *Trist.* IV. vii. 21—

'Innumeri montes inter me teque, viæque,
  Fluminaque et campi, nec freta pauca jacent.'

125] Keightley is mistaken in supposing that 'vestri' ought to be 'vestrum.' Zumpt, in his Latin Grammar (§ 431 of Schmitz' translation), draws the distinction thus: 'The forms ending in *-um* are used as partitive genitives, e.g. *uterque nostrum*, &c.; but *miserere nostri*, &c.' He notes however that *vestrum* does occur 'without any partitive meaning, e.g. "frequentia vestrum incredibilis," Cic. *in Rull.* ii. 21; but these are exceptional cases.'

126] See note on *l.* 13.

127 Tuscus] See on Diodati's family in the Introduction to *Lycidas*.

128] Lucca was said to have been founded by Lucumon, an Etruscan king. During his second visit to Florence, Milton visited the place, no doubt on account of its connexion with Diodati (Masson, *Life of Milton*, vol. i. p. 771).

132 certantem] i.e. at the 'private academies' referred to on *l.* 13. 'Lycidas' and 'Menalcas' are of course pastoral names for members of these societies; not 'unknown,' as Keightley asserts, for Milton, in the sketch of his own life quoted above, enumerates Gaddi, Frescobaldi, Coltellini, Buonmattei, and Chimentelli, besides Dati and Francini, who are mentioned below

Ipse etiam tentare ausus sum ; nec, puto, multum
Displicui ; nam sunt et apud me, munera vestra,
Fiscellæ calathique, et cerea vincla cicutæ :   135
Quin et nostra suas docuerunt nomina fagos
Et Datis et Francinus, erant et vocibus ambo
Et studiis noti, Lydorum sanguinis ambo.
 Ite domum impasti, domino jam non vacat, agni.
Hæc mihi tum læto dictabat roscida luna,   140
Dum solus teneros claudebam cratibus hædos.
Ah quoties dixi, cum te cinis ater habebat,
Nunc canit aut lepori nunc tendit retia Damon,
Vimina nunc texit, varios sibi quod sit in usus !
Et quæ tum facili sperabam mente futura   145
Arripui voto levis et præsentia finxi ;
'Heus bone ! numquid agis? nisi te quid forte retardat,
 Imus ? et arguta paulum recubamus in umbra,

(*l.* 137). Professor Masson (vol. i. p. 722 foll.) has given a full and detailed account of every one of them. On what follows, he remarks (vol. ii. p. 90, note) that there is 'a distinct reference to the two written encomiums by Dati and Francini,' and that the 'fiscellæ,' &c., are doubtless 'poetical names for little presents actually received from Florentine friends.'

135 **cerea vincla cicutæ**] = 'cicuta cereis vinculis compacta,' Virg. *E.* ii. 32, 36.

136 **docuerunt, &c.**] Cf. Virg. *E.* i. 5.

138] For the tradition about the Lydian origin of the Etruscans, see Herod. i. 94: Τυρσηνὸν... ἀποπλέειν κατὰ βίου τε καὶ γῆς ζήτησιν, ἐς ὃ ἀπικέσθαι ἐς 'Ομβρικούς, ἔνθα ἐνιδρύσασθαι πόλιας. Virg. *Æn.* viii. 479, 'ubi *Lydia* quondam Gens bello præclara jugis insedit Etruscis.' Warton refers to Hor. *Sat.* I. vi. 1.

140 **hæc**] i.e. the thoughts expressed in *l.* 143 foll.

roscida luna] Virg. *G.* iii. 337. Warton compares *Lycidas*, 29, and for 'cratibus' the 'wattled cotes' in *Comus*, 345, and Hor. *Epod.* ii..45, 'claudensque textis cratibus lætum pecus.'

142 **cinis ater**] a confusion between the mould of the grave and the ashes of the dead ; for which, however, Milton has the authority of Virgil, *Æn.* iv. 633.

144] Virg. *E.* ii. 71 :
'Quin tu aliquid saltem potius *quorum indiget usus*
Viminibus mollique paras *detexere* junco.'

Possibly 'paras' in this passage may have induced Milton to write 'imus' and 'recubamus' (*l.* 148) where we should expect 'eamus' and 'recubemus,' or else the future ; since it is doubtful whether the *pres. ind.* can be so used without the 'quin.' As, how-

'Aut ad aquas Colni aut ubi jugera Cassibelauni?
'Tu mihi percurres medicos, tua gramina, succos, 150
'Helleborumque humilesque crocos foliumque hyacinthi,
'Quasque habet ista palus herbas artesque medentum.'
Ah pereant herbæ, pereant artesque medentum,
Gramina postquam ipsi nil profecere magistro!
Ipse etiam, nam nescio quid mihi grande sonabat 155
Fistula, ab undecima jam lux est altera nocte,

ever, *ire* (like ἰέναι) has in itself the sense of the future, 'imus' might be allowed to stand, and the actual form of its tense may have influenced that of the other verb.

149] The river Colne flows by Horton (see on *l.* 3). 'Jugera Cassibelauni' are the district of St. Albans, the dominions of the British king Cassibelaun. Cf. Cæsar, *B. G.* v. 11, 'Cassivellauno, cujus fines a maritimis civitatibus flumen dividit quod appellatur Tamesis.'

150 foll.] in allusion to Diodati's practice of medicine (see Introduction to *Lycidas*). He is the 'shepherd-lad' in *Comus*, 619, 'well skilled In every virtuous plant and healing herb.' There is a characteristic passage bearing upon this subject in Milton's letter to Diodati dated Sept. 23, 1637: 'You wish me good health six hundred times, which is as much as I can desire, or even more. Surely you must lately have been appointed the very steward of Health's larder (*salutis condum promum*), so lavishly do you dispense all her stores, or at least Health should now certainly be your parasite, since you so lord it over her (*pro rege te geris*), and command her to attend your bidding.'

153] Todd quotes the words of Phœbus to Daphne, Ovid, *Met.* i. 524, 'nec prosunt domino quæ prosunt omnibus artes.'

155-178] For a detailed examination of this interesting passage consult Masson, vol. ii. pp. 93-97. The two main points to be noticed are: (1) That Milton was already (in 1639) forming a plan of writing a British epic, which should extend from the legendary times of the Trojan Brutus to the reign of King Arthur; (2) That he had determined henceforth to write no more in Latin, but in English, so as to be read by all his countrymen from the Thames to the Humber, and from Cornwall to the Orkneys. This idea had occurred to him even while in Italy, and was fostered, if not first suggested, by the compliments of his Florentine friends upon his former productions;—'that by labour and intent study, joined with the strong propensity of nature, I might perhaps leave something so written to aftertimes, as they should not willingly let it die' (*Reason of Church Government*, B. ii.). He soon afterwards abandoned the project in favour of a poem on a Scriptural subject, which ultimately took the form of the *Paradise Lost*, the materials he had collected for the British Epic being employed in his *History of Britain*, about 1649 or 1650.

155 **grande, &c.**] Cf. 'the strain of higher mood,' *Lycidas*, 87.

156] From Virg. *E.* viii. 39, 'alter ab undecimo tum jam me acceperat annus;' where Conington

Et tum forte novis admoram labra cicutis,
Dissiluere tamen rupta compage, nec ultra
Ferre graves potuere sonos : dubito quoque ne sim
Turgidulus, tamen et referam ; vos cedite silvæ.   160
    Ite domum impasti, domino jam non vacat, agni.
Ipse ego Dardanias Rutupina per æquora puppes
Dicam, et Pandrasidos regnum vetus Imogeniæ,
Brennumque Arviragumque duces, priscumque Belinum,
Et tandem Armoricos Britonum sub lege colonos ;   165
Tum gravidam Arturo fatali fraude Iogernen,
Mendaces vultus assumptaque Gorlois arma,

remarks that the twelfth, and not the thirteenth, is meant, according to the 'inclusive mode of counting.'

159 graves] applied both literally to the low tones of the pipe, and metaphorically to the dignity of the subject. Cowper's translation, 'the deep-toned music of the solemn strain,' well expresses both these ideas.

160 turgidulus] inflated with pride ; but this use of the word is barely classical, though 'turgida oratio' is said of a 'bombastic speech.'

cedite silvæ] Cf. Virg. *E.* x. 63, where Gallus bids farewell to a woodland life, because it cannot cure his passion, with the words 'concedite silvæ.'

162 foll.] For the legends connected with each of these names, see Milton's *History of Britain*, B. i. ii., and Geoffrey of Monmouth, whence he derived the account. Brutus the Trojan, having rescued his countrymen from their servile condition under the Grecian prince *Pandrasus*, marries his daughter *Imogen*, and sets sail with his followers towards the west. He finally lands in Britain, on what is now the Kentish coast (*Rutupina æquora*), and establishes a kingdom. *Bren-*

nus and *Belinus* are the sons of Dunwallo Molmutius, king of Cornwall. Some twenty generations after Brutus, *Arviragus*, son of Cunobelin (Cymbeline), by personating his slain brother Guiderius, is said to have gained a victory over the Roman emperor Claudius. The 'Armorici coloni' were Britons who fled from the Saxon invaders in the time of Vortigern to Armorica, now Bretagne. The last legend (found in Geoffrey of Monmouth, but not told by Milton in his own History) is that of Uther Pendragon, who by Merlin's magic art assumed the form of Gorlois, king of Cornwall, and thus obtained access to his wife Iogerne at Tintagel Castle, by whom he became the father of the famous Arthur.

165] Cf. *P. L.* i. 581. Armorica was peopled in the fourth century by a Welsh colony, under the Roman general Maximus and Carron, prince of Meiriadoc or Denbighland. Thierry (*Norman Conquest*, B. i. p. 16) says : 'They found people of their own stock there, and this agglomeration of branches of the Keltic race and language preserved that western nook of France from the irruption of the Roman tongue.'

EPITAPHIUM DAMONIS.

Merlini dolus.   O mihi tum si vita supersit,
Tu procul annosa pendebis, fistula, pinu,.
Multum oblita mihi ; aut patriis mutata Camenis   •   170
Brittonicum strides, quid enim ? omnia non licet uni,
Non sperasse uni licet omnia, mi satis ampla
Merces, et mihi grande decus (sim ignotus in ævum
Tum licet, externo penitusque inglorius orbi,)
Si me flava comas legat Usa et potor Alauni,   175
Vorticibusque frequens Abra et nemus omne Treantæ,
Et Thamesis meus ante omnes et fusca metallis
Tamara, et extremis me discant Orcades undis.
   Ite domum impasti, domino jam non vacat, agni.

169] Virg. *E.* vii. 24, 'Hic arguta sacra pendebis fistula pinu,' a sign that he intended to sing no more. The sense should therefore be, 'Either I will abandon poetry altogether, or else change it from Latin verse into English.' But if Prof. Masson is right in explaining 'fistula' of *Latin* poetry in particular, the alternative 'aut—aut' is merely formal, the real meaning being this : 'I will abandon Latin verse for English.' 'Patriis Camenis' will then signify '*its* native Muse,' i.e. the Latin.

171 **strides**] in reference to the rougher warlike themes he was about to celebrate. See Masson's translation, 'the British war-screech,' and compare the lines prefixed to Virgil's *Æneid,* 'Ille ego . . . at nunc horrentia Martis.' 'Strides' is the future of *strido*, a form which occurs in Virg. *Æn.* iv. 689; viii. 420 ; Ovid, *Met.* ix. 171, &c.

172] Virg. *E.* vii. 23, 'non omnia possumus omnes.'

173 **in ævum**] 'for all time,' Hor. *Od.* IV. xiv. 3.

175 **Usa**] the Ouse ; but whether the Bucks or the Yorkshire river is here intended is uncertain. The former supposition is slightly supported by the fact of Milton's residence in Buckinghamshire ; while on the other hand the names of the rivers immediately following seem to point to a northern locality. Keightley, who adopts the latter view, refers to the *Vacation Exercise, l.* 92, where the Ouse is mentioned in company with the Tweed, Don, and Trent. The epithet 'flava comas,' which applies generally to the Saxon race, does not help towards deciding the question. The other rivers are the Alan in Northumberland, the Humber (properly 'Abus'), Trent, Thames, and Tamar in Cornwall, hence 'fusca metallis.' With 'potor Alauni' cf. Hor. *Od.* II. xx. 20, 'Rhodanique potor,' also IV. xv. 21, 'qui Tanain bibunt.'

176] 'Treanta' seems to be formed from the modern name of the river ; the Romans called it *Trivona.*

177 **Thamesis meus**] Keightley compares Spenser, *F. Q.* IV. xi. 41, 'And Mulla *mine* whose waves I whilom taught to weep.'

Hæc tibi servabam lenta sub cortice lauri, 180
Hæc et plura simul; tum quæ mihi pocula Mansus,
Mansus Chalcidicæ non ultima gloria ripæ,
Bina dedit, mirum artis opus, mirandus et ipse,

180 hæc] probably refers to the British poem, which when completed he intended to submit to his friend for criticism. Thus in the 6th Elegy (*ll.* 79 foll.) he tells Diodati that he has been writing a hymn upon the Nativity, upon which he will ask his opinion—

'Te quoque pressa manent patriis
  meditata cicutis;
Tu mihi cui recitem judicis instar
  eris.'

See also his letter of Sept. 23, 1637, containing an account of the studies in which he was then engaged.

181-197] On the strength of this passage, Prof. Masson (adopting a suggestion of Warton's) asserts that Manso had actually given Milton a pair of chased goblets. Keightley on the other hand considers it to be merely a poetical description after Theocritus (*Id.* i. 27 foll.) and Virgil (*E.* iii. 36 foll.) of some other tokens of Manso's esteem. All we know for certain is that he had sent Milton a complimentary elegiac couplet—

'Ut mens forma decor facies mos,
  si pietas sic,
Non Anglus, verum hercle An-
  gelus ipse fores.'

Also in the account of his travels, to which we have before referred, Milton says that Manso 'gave him singular proofs of his regard,' which may reasonably be supposed to have taken some tangible form; the more so, because it is further stated that Manso had excused himself for not paying him greater personal attention, on account of his free speaking on religious matters. With all due deference to Mr. Keightley's opinion, as to the inherent *improbability* of the matter, we should be disposed to say that a pair of silver cups would be a very likely present from a wealthy Neapolitan *virtuoso* to his English friend; nor is this likelihood really diminished by the mere fact of similar representations in Theocritus and Virgil, especially when we bear in mind that no part of the details of Milton's description is in any way borrowed from theirs. And when we proceed to examine these details further, both the singularity of the subjects chosen and the minuteness of each point in the picture render it almost impossible to suppose that we have here a mere invention of the poet, and not an actual thing described. It is of course barely possible that such may have been the case, but the probability seems to lie very strongly the other way.

182] Naples (Neapolis) was founded by the Cumæans, who were originally colonists from Chalcis in Eubœa. Cf. Livy. viii. 22, 'Cumani ab Chalcide Euboica originem trahunt.' Hence the rock of Cumæ is called 'Chalcidica arx' in Virg. *Æn.* vi. 17. Milton may have purposely used the older name in recognition of the antiquity of Manso's family. Cf. 'Lydorum sanguinis ambo,' *l.* 138 *supra*. Warton curiously quotes 'Chalcidico versu,' Virg. *E.* x. 50, which alludes to Euphorion, a poet of Chalcis, but has nothing to do either with Cumæ or with Naples.

Et circum gemino cælaverat argumento :
In medio rubri maris unda et odoriferum ver,   185
Littora longa Arabum et sudantes balsama silvæ ;
Has inter Phœnix, divina avis, unica terris,
Cæruleum fulgens diversicoloribus alis,
Auroram vitreis surgentem respicit undis ;
Parte alia polus omnipatens et magnus Olympus :   190
Quis putet ? hic quoque Amor pictæque in nube pharetræ,
Arma corusca faces, et spicula tincta pyropo ;
Nec tenues animas pectusque ignobile vulgi,
Hinc ferit ; at circum flammantia lumina torquens
Semper in erectum spargit sua tela per orbes   195
Impiger, et pronos nunquam collimat ad ictus :

184 **cælaverat argumento**] Ovid, *Met.* xiii. 68*f*. 4

187] For the fable of the Phœnix see Ovid, *Met.* xv. 391 foll. ; *Amor.* II. vi. 54 ; Pliny, *Nat. Hist.* x. ii. 2.

unica terris] Cf. *P. L.* v. 272, 'that *sole* bird.'

188] 'Diversicolor' is post-classical ; the regular word is *versicolor*, Virg. *Æn.* x. 181 ; Livy, XXXIV. i. 3, &c.

190 **omnipatens**] seems to be a word of Milton's own coining.

191. **Quis putet ?**] expressing admiration ; something like the Greek πῶς δοκεῖς ; as in Aristoph. *Nubes*, 881, ἐκ τῶν σιδίων βατράχους ἐποίει, πῶς δοκεῖς ;

192] If 'arma corusca faces' is the right reading, it can only mean 'arms gleaming with [the light of] his torches.' But this is a very bold use of the so-called Greek accusative, and one which no existing expression in any Latin writer seems to justify. Perhaps the nearest approach to it is to be found in Hor. *Ep.* I. vi. 74, 'Pueri suspensi loculos tabulamque ;' but this may be explained as a mere variety of the ordinary phrases 'indutus vestem,' &c., which will hardly include the instance before us. The insertion of a comma after 'corusca,' thus making 'faces' the nominative, would remove the difficulty ; but I have not ventured to introduce this change of punctuation into the text.

pyropo] a kind of bronze, of a fiery red colour, named from πύρωπος, which is an epithet of the lightning-bolt in Æsch. *Prom.* 667. Cf. Ovid, *Met.* ii. 2, 'flammas imitante pyropo.' In *Met.* i. 469 Cupid is described with two darts, one tipped with gold, the other with lead—

'fugat hoc, facit illud amorem.
Quod facit auratum est, et cuspide
   fulget acuta ;
Quod fugat obtusum est, et habet
   sub arundine plumbum.'

195 **in erectum**] the neuter adj. used substantively, 'into an elevated region.' Cf. 'per arduum,' Hor. *Od.* II. xix. 21.

per orbes] 'among the stars' (Warton).

Hinc mentes ardere sacræ formæque deorum.
  Tu quoque in his, nec me fallit spes lubrica, Damon,
Tu quoque in his certe es, nam quo tua dulcis abiret
Sanctaque simplicitas, nam quo tua candida virtus?   200
Nec te Lethæo fas quæsivisse sub orco,
Nec tibi conveniunt lacrimæ, nec flebimus ultra:
Ite procul, lacrimæ; purum colit æthera Damon,
Æthera purus habet, pluvium pede reppulit arcum;
Heroumque animas inter divosque perennes   205
Æthereos haurit latices, et gaudia potat
Ore sacro.   Quin tu, cœli post jura recepta,
Dexter ades placidusque fave quicunque vocaris,
Seu tu noster eris Damon, sive æquior audis

196 *collimat*] 'takes aim.' The word *collimare* is now understood not to exist; it was formerly found in editions of Cicero, Gellius, &c., the supposed meaning being 'to look *sidelong* at anything' (as if from the adj. *limus*), but it has been expunged everywhere as a mistake for *collineare*, 'to aim in a straight line.'

197] Keightley remarks that 'divine, not sensual love is here spoken of.' See *P. L.* viii. 592; *Comus*, 1004; Quarles, *Emblems*, ii. 8. Milton was doubtless familiar with the magnificent description of Celestial Love in Plato's *Symposium* (c. 8) and *Phædrus* (c. 30 foll.).

198-219] The mention of 'sacred minds and forms divine' leads the poet to describe that state of heavenly bliss which he is assured that the soul of his friend is now enjoying. This passage will bear a close comparison with that in *Lycidas*, 165 foll., both as regards the general sentiment and some particular expressions; there is the same juxtaposition of classical and Scriptural imagery, only here the former largely predominates, as might be expected from the form of the poem and the language in which it is written. The apotheosis of Daphnis in Virgil's 5th Eclogue seems to have been chiefly before Milton's mind on both occasions.

200 **sancta simplicitas**] Cf. *l.* 33.

201 **quæsivisse**] The perfect tense has great force here. The first impulse of grief was to mourn the departed one as lost and gone, but it is presently rejected for an expression of belief in his immortality. See *Lycidas*, 165, 166, 204; Virg. *E.* v. 56, 57. The fine idea of springing upwards from the arc of the rainbow is partly due to Virgil, *G.* iv. 233, where the rising Pleiad is said to 'spurn with her foot the Ocean stream' ('Oceani spretos pede reppulit amnes').

205] Keightley comp. Hor. *Od.* III. iii. 11, 'Quos inter Augustus recumbens Purpureo bibit ore nectar.'

208] See note and reff. on *Lycidas*, 184.

209 **audis**] as in Hor. *Sat.* II. vi. 20, 'seu Jane libentius audis.' Different names of a god implied

Diodatus, quo te divino nomine cuncti 210
Cœlicolæ norint, silvisque vocabere Damon.
Quod tibi purpureus pudor et sine labe juventus
Grata fuit, quod nulla tori libata voluptas,
En etiam tibi virginei servantur honores;
Ipse caput nitidum cinctus rutilante corona, 215
Lætaque frondentis gestans umbracula palmæ,
Æternum perages immortales hymenæos;
Cantus ubi choreisque furit lyra mista beatis,
Festa Sionæo bacchantur et Orgia thyrso.

different attributes (Exodus vi. 3); whence arose the idea that one name would on certain occasions be more acceptable than another. Thus the Chorus in Æsch. *Agam.* 155 exclaims: Ζεὺς, ὅστις ποτ' ἐστίν, εἰ τόδ αὐτῷ φίλον κεκλημένῳ, τοῦτό νιν προσεννέπω.

210 **Diodatus**] 'God-given,' hence '*divino* nomine.' One of Diodati's letters begins with the words Θεοδότος Μίλτωνι χαίρειν (see Introduction, p. 31).

211 **silvis**] i.e. by us shepherds.

212] Richardson comp. Ovid, *Amor.* I. iii. 14, 'Nudaque simplicitas purpureusque pudor.' The latter is the rosy blush of modesty; cf. Virg. *Æn.* i. 591, 'lumenque juventæ Purpureum' (see note on *Lycidas*, 141).

214] Warton observes that Diodati was unmarried, and quotes Rev. xiv. 3, 4. Cf. also Bp. Taylor, *Holy Living*, xi. 3 (quoted by Keble in the *Christian Year*, Wednesday before Easter), 'that little coronet or special reward, which God hath prepared for those "who have not defiled themselves with women, but follow the Lamb for ever."'

216 **palmæ**] Rev. vii. 9.

217 **hymenæos**] See *Lycidas*, 176 and note.

219 **thyrso**] the instrumental ablative, 'under the inspiration of the thyrsus,' the instrument which excited the Bacchantes to phrensy. We have here perhaps the most startling instance to be found in Milton's poetry of that blending of sacred with pagan imagery, to which reference has so often been made. Such a conception as is here presented to us can only be accounted for (and even then not wholly excused) on the hypothesis that partly from the custom of the period, partly from his own literary associations, the images derived from classical mythology had become so familiar to Milton's mind that their precise original import was for the time forgotten. To suppose that he would seriously have admitted any real comparison between the orgies of Dionysus and the joys of the saints in glory would be to contradict all that we know, from other sources, of his genuine piety and the intense sincerity of his devotion.

TRANSLATION OF THE EPITAPHIUM DAMONIS.

By Charles Symmons, D.D. Jesus Coll. Oxon., 1806.

Damon, an Epitaphial Elegy.

Ye nymphs of Himera (whose stream along
The notes have floated of your mournful song,
As Daphnis or as Hylas you deplored,
Or Bion, once the shepherds' tuneful lord;)
Lend your Sicilian softness to proclaim 5
The woes of Thyrsis on the banks of Thame;
What plaints he murmured to the springs and floods,
How waked the sorrowing echoes of the woods,
As frantic for his Damon lost, alone
He roamed, and taught the sleepless night to groan. 10
Twice the green blade had bristled on the plain,
And twice the golden car enriched the swain,
Since Damon by a doom too strict expired,
And his pale eye his absent friend required.
For Thyrsis still his wished return delayed; 15
The Muses held him in the Tuscan shade.
But when with satiate taste and careful thought
His long-forgotten home and flock he sought,
Ah! then, beneath the accustomed elm reclined,
All—all his loss came rushing to his mind. 20
Undone and desolate, for transient ease
He poured his swelling heart in strains like these:
   Return unfed, my lambs; by fortune crost
   Your hapless master now to you is lost!
What powers shall I of earth or heaven invoke, 25
Since Damon fell by their relentless stroke?

And shalt thou leave us thus? and shall thy worth
Sleep in a nameless grave with common earth?
But he whose wand the realms of death controls
Forbids thy shade to blend with common souls. 30
While these o'erawed disperse at his command,
He leads thee to thy own distinguished band.
 Return unfed, my lambs; by fortune crost
 Your hapless master now to you is lost!
And sure, unless beneath some evil eye, 35
That blights me with its glance, my powers should die,
Thou shalt not slumber on thy timeless bier
'Without the meed of one melodious tear.'
Long shall thy name, thy virtues long remain
In fond memorial with the shepherd train; 40
Their festive honours and their votive lay
To thee, as to their Daphnis, they shall pay,—
Their Daphnis thou, as long as Pales loves
The springing meads, or Faunus haunts the groves;
If aught of power or faith and truth attend, 45
Palladian science and a Muse thy friend.
 Return unfed, my lambs; by fortune crost
 Your hapless master now to you is lost!
Yes, Damon, thee such recompenses wait.—
But ah! what ills hang gloomy o'er my fate? 50
Who now, still faithful to my side, will bear
Keen frosts or suns that parch the sickening air,
When boldly, to protect the distant fold,
We seek the growling savage in his hold?
Who now, as we retrace the long rough way, 55
With tale or song will soothe the weary day?
 Return unfed, my lambs; by fortune crost
 Your hapless master now to you is lost!
To whom my bosom shall I now confide?
At whose soft voice will now my cares subside? 60
Who now will cheat the night with harmless mirth,
As the nut crackles on the glowing hearth,
Or the pear hisses,—while without the storm
Roars through the wood and ruffles nature's form?
 Return unfed, my lambs; by fortune crost 65
 Your hapless master now to you is lost!
In summer too, at noontide's sultry hour,

When Pan lies sleeping in his beechen bower;
When diving from the day's oppressive heat
The panting Naiad seeks her crystal seat;   70
When every shepherd leaves the silent plain,
And the green hedge protects the snoring swain;
Whose playful fancy then shall light the smile?
Whose Attic tongue relieve my languid toil?
   Return unfed, my lambs; by fortune crost   75
   Your hapless master now to you is lost!
Ah! now through meads and vales alone I stray,
Or linger sad where woods embrown the day;
As drives the storm, and Eurus o'er my head
Breaks the loose twilight of the billowy shade.   80
   Return unfed, my lambs; by fortune crost
   Your hapless master now to you is lost!
My late trim fields their laboured culture scorn,
And idle weeds insult my drooping corn;
My widowed vine in prone dishonour sees   85
Her clusters wither;—not a shrub can please.
E'en my sheep tire me; they with upward eyes
Gaze at my grief, and seem to feel my sighs.
   Return unfed, my lambs; by fortune crost
   Your hapless master now to you is lost!   90
My shepherd friends, by various tastes inclined,
Direct my steps the sweetest spot to find.
This likes the hazel, *that* the beechen grove;
One bids me here, one there for pleasure rove.
Aegon the willow's pensile shade delights,   95
And gay Amyntas to the streams invites.
' Here are cool fountains; here is mossy grass;
' Here zephyrs softly whisper as they pass.
' From this light spring yon arbute draws her green,
' The pride and beauty of the sylvan scene.'   100
Deaf is my woe, and while they speak in vain,
I plunge into the copse and hide my pain.
   Return unfed, my lambs; by fortune crost
   Your hapless master now to you is lost!
Mopsus surprised me in my sullen mood,   105
(Mopsus who knew the language of the wood;
Knew all the stars, could all their junctions spell.)
And thus;—' What passions in your bosom swell?

EPITAPHIUM DAMONIS.

'Speak! flows the poison from disastrous love?
'Or falls the mischief star-sent from above?' 110
'For leaden Saturn, with his chill control,
'Oft has shot blights into the shepherd's soul.'
 Return unfed, my lambs; by fortune crost
 Your hapless master now to you is lost!
The wandering nymphs exclaim—'What, Thyrsis, now? 115
'Those heavy eyelids and that cloudy brow
'Become not youth; to youth the jocund song,
'Frolic and dance and wanton wiles belong.
'With these he courts the joys that suit his state;
'Ah! twice unhappy he who loves too late!' 120
 Return unfed, my lambs; by fortune crost
 Your hapless master now to you is lost!
With Dryope and Hyas, Ægle came,
A lovely lyrist, but a scornful dame.
From Chelmer's banks fair Chloris joined the train; 125
But vain their blandishments, their solace vain.
Dead is my hope, and pointless beauty's dart
To waken torpid pleasure in my heart.
 Return unfed, my lambs; by fortune crost
 Your hapless master now to you is lost! 130
How blest where, none repulsed and none preferred,
One common friendship blends the lowing herd!
Touched by no subtle magnet in the mind,
Each meets a comrade when he meets his kind.
Conspiring wolves enjoy this equal love, 135
And this the zebra's parti-coloured drove;
This too the tribes of ocean, and the flock
Which Proteus feeds beneath his vaulted rock.
The sparrow, fearless of a lonely state,
Has ever for his social wing a mate; 140
Whom should the falcon or the marksman strike,
He soon repairs his loss and finds a like.
But we, by Fate's severer frown oppressed,
With war and sharp repulsion in the breast,
Can scarcely meet amid the human throng 145
One kindred soul, or met preserve him long.
When fortune, now determined to be kind,
Yields the rich gift, and mind is linked to mind,

Death mocks the fond possession, bursts the chain,
And plants the bosom with perennial pain. 150
   Return unfed, my lambs; by fortune crost
   Your hapless master now to you is lost:
Alas! what madness tempted me to stray
Where other suns on distant regions play?
To tread aerial paths and Alpine snows, 155
Scared by stern Nature's terrible repose?
Ah! could the sepulchre of buried Rome
Thus urge my frantic foot to spurn my home?
Though Rome were now, as once in pomp arrayed
She drew the Mantuan from his flock and shade; 160
Ah! could she lure me from thy faithful side,
Lead me where rocks would part us, floods divide,
Forests and lofty mountains intervene,
Whole realms extend and oceans roar between?
Ah, wretch! denied to press thy fainting hand, 165
Close thy dim eyes and catch thy last command;
To say—' My friend, O think of all our love,
' And bear it glowing to the realms above!'
   Return unfed, my lambs; by fortune crost
   Your hapless master now to you is lost! 170
Yet must I not deplore the hours that flew,
Ye Tuscan swains, with science and with you;—
' Each Grace and Muse is yours,'—and yours my Damon too.
From ancient Lucca's Tuscan walls he came,
With you in country, talents, arts the same. 175
How happy, lulled by Arno's warbling stream,
Hid by his poplars from day's flaring beam,
When stretched along the fragrant moss I lay,
And culled the violet or plucked the bay;
Or heard, contending for the rural prize, 180
Famed Lycid's and Menalcas' melodies.
I too essayed to sing, nor vainly sung;
This flute, these baskets speak my victor tongue—
And Datis and Francinus, swains who trace
Their Tuscan lineage to the Lydian race, 185
Dear to the Muses both, with friendly care
Taught their carved trees my favoured name to bear.
   Return unfed, my lambs; by fortune crost
   Your hapless master now to you is lost!

Then, as the moonbeam slumbered on the plain,   190
I penned my fold, and sung in cheerful strain;
And oft exclaimed, unconscious of my doom,
As your pale ashes mouldered in the tomb—
'Now he is singing; now my friend prepares
'His twisted osiers or his wiry snares!'   195
Then would rash fancy on the future seize,
And hail you present in such words as these—
'What? loitering here? unless some cause dissuade,
'Haste and enjoy with me the whispering shade;
'Or where his course the lucid Colnus bends,   200
'Or where Cassibelan's domain extends.
'There shew what herbs in vale or upland grow,
'The harebell's ringlet and the saffron's glow;
'There teach me all the physic of the plains,
'What healing virtues swell the floret's veins.'   205
Ah! perish all the healing plants, confest
Too weak to save the swain who knew them best!
As late a new-compacted pipe I found,
It gave beneath my lips a loftier sound;
Too high indeed the notes; for as it spoke   210
The waxen junctures in the labour broke.
Smile as you may, I will not hide from you
The ambitious strain;—ye woods, awhile adieu!
 Return unfed, my lambs; by fortune crost
 Your hapless master now to you is lost!   215
High on Rutupium's cliffs my muse shall hail
The first white gleamings of the Dardan sail;
Shall sing the realms by Imogen controlled,
And Brennus, Arvirage, and Belin old;
Shall sing Armorica at length subdued   220
By British steel in Gallic blood imbrued;
And Uther in the form of Gorlois led
By Merlin's fraud to Iogerne's bed,
Whence Arthur sprang. If length of days be mine,
My shepherd's pipe shall hang on yon old pine   225
In long neglect; or tuned to British strains
With British airs shall please my native swains.
But wherefore so? alas! no human mind
Can hope for audience all the human kind.

Enough for me ; I ask no more renown   230
(Lost to the world, to Britain only known),
If yellow-tressèd Usa read my lays,
Alain and gulphy Humber sound my praise,
Trent's sylvan echoes answer to my song,
My own dear Thames my warbled notes prolong ; 235
Ore-tinctured Tamar own me for her bard,
And Thule mid her utmost flood regard.
    Return unfed, my lambs; by fortune crost
    Your hapless master now to you is lost !
These lays, and more like these, for thee designed   240
I wrote, and folded in the laurel's rind.
For thee I also kept, of antique mould,
Two spacious goblets, rough with laboured gold.
(Rare was the gift, but yet the giver more,
Mansus the pride of the Chalcidian shore).   245
In bold existence, from the workman's hand,
Two subjects on their fretted surface stand.
Here by the Red Sea coast, in length displayed,
Arabia pants beneath her odorous shade ;
And here the Phœnix from his spicy throne,   250
In heavenly plumage radiant and alone,
Himself a kind, beholds with flamy sight
The wave first kindle with the morning light.
There on another side the heavens unfold,
And great Olympus shines in brighter gold.   255
Strange though it seems, conspicuous on the scene
The god of love displays his infant mien ;
Dazzling his arms, his quiver, torch and bow,
His brilliant shafts with points of topaz glow.
With these he meditates no common wound,   260
But proudly throws a fiery glance around ;
And scorning vulgar aims, directs on high
His war against the people of the sky ;
Thence struck with sacred flame the ethereal race
Rush to new joys, and heavenly minds embrace. 265
    With these is Damon now, my hope is sure ;
Yes ! with the just, the holy and the pure,
My Damon dwells ;—'twere impious to surmise
Virtues like his could rest below the skies.

THE SAME

By Professor Masson, 1873.—Reprinted from his 'Life of Milton,' Vol. II. p. 85.

On the Death of Damon.

The Argument.

THYRSIS and DAMON, shepherds of the same neighbourhood, following the same pursuits, were friends from their boyhood, in the highest degree of mutual attachment. Thyrsis, having set out to travel for mental improvement, received news when abroad of Damon's death. Afterwards at length returning, and finding the matter to be so, he deplores himself and his solitary condition in the following poem. Under the guise of Damon, however, is here understood Charles Diodati, tracing his descent on the father's side from the Tuscan city of Lucca, but otherwise English—a youth remarkable, while he lived, for his genius, his learning, and other most shining virtues.

NYMPHS of old Himera's stream (for ye it was that remembered
Daphnis and Hylas when dead, and grieved for the sad fate of Bion),
Tell through the hamlets of Thames this later Sicilian story—
What were the cries and murmurs that burst from Thyrsis the
    wretched,
What lamentations continued he wrung from the caves and the
    rivers,
Wrung from the wandering brooks and the grove's most secret
    recesses,
Mourning his Damon lost, and compelling even the midnight
Into the sound of his woe, as he wandered in desolate places.
Twice had the ears in the wheat-fields shot through the green of
    their sheathing,
As many crops of pale gold were the reapers counting as garnered,
Since the last day that had taken Damon down from the living,

Then cease our tears! from his superior seat 270
He sees the showery arch beneath his feet;
And mixed with heroes and with gods above
Quaffs endless draughts of life, and joy and love.
But thou, when fixed on thy empyreal throne,
When heaven's eternal rights are all thy own, 275
O still attend us from thy starry sphere,
Still as we call thee by thy name most dear,
Diodatus above—but yet our Damon here!
As thine was roseate purity, that fled
In youth abstemious from the nuptial bed, 280
Thy virgin triumphs heavenly spousals wait;—
Lo! where it leads along its festal state;
A crown of living lustre binds thy brow,
Thy hand sustains the palm's immortal bough;
While the full song, the dance, the frantic lyre, 285
And Sion's thyrsus wildly waved conspire
To solemnise the rites, and boundless joys inspire.

Thyrsis not being by; for then that shepherd was absent,
Kept by the Muse's sweet love in the far-famed town of the Tuscan.
But, when his satiate mind, and the care of his flock recollected,
Brought him back to his home, and he sat, as of old, 'neath the elm-tree,
Then at last, O then, as the sense of his loss comes upon him,
Thus he begins to disburthen all his measureless sorrow :—
  Go unpastured, my lambs: your master now heeds not your bleating.
Ah me ! what deities now shall I call on in earth or in heaven,
After the pitiless death by which they have reft thee, my Damon?
Thus dost thou leave us? thus without name is thy virtue departed
Down to the world below, to take rank with the shadows unnoted?
No! May He that disparteth souls with his glittering baton
Will it not so, but lead thee into some band of the worthies,
Driving far from thy side all the mere herd of the voiceless !
  Go unpastured, my lambs: your master now heeds not your bleating.
Hap as it may, unless the wolf's black glance shall first cross me,
Not in a tearless tomb shall thy loved mortality moulder ;
Stand shall thine honour for thee, and long henceforth shall it flourish
Mid our shepherd-lads ; and thee they shall joy to remember
Next after Daphnis chief, next after Daphnis to praise thee,
So long as Pales and Faunus shall love our fields and our meadows,
If it avails to have cherished the faith of the old and the loyal,
Pallas's arts of peace, and have had a tuneful companion !
  Go unpastured, my lambs: your master now heeds not your bleating.
Kept are these honours for thee, and thine they *shall* be, my Damon !
But for myself what remains ? For me what faithful companion
Now will cling to my side, in the place of the one so familiar,
All through the season harsh when the grounds are crisp with the snow-crust,
Or 'neath the blazing sun when the herbage is dying for moisture ?
Were it the task to go forth in the track of the ravaging lions,
Or to drive back from the folds the wolf-packs boldened by hunger,
Who would now lighten the day with the sound of his talk or his singing ?

EPITAPHIUM DAMONIS.

 Go unpastured, my lambs: your master now heeds not your bleating.
Whom shall I trust with my thoughts; or who will teach me to deaden
Heart-hid pains; or who will cheat away the long evening
Sweetly with chat by the fire, where hissing hot on the ashes
Roasts the ripe pear, and the chestnuts crackle beneath, while the South-wind
Hurls confusion without, and thunders down on the elm-tops?
 Go unpastured, my lambs: your master now heeds not your bleating.
Then, in the summer, when day spins round on his middlemost axle,
What time Pan takes his sleep concealed in the shade of the beeches,
And when the nymphs have repaired to their well-known grots in the rivers,
Shepherds are not to be seen and under the hedge snores the rustic,
Who will bring me again thy blandishing ways and thy laughter,
All thy Athenian jests, and all the fine wit of thy fancies?
 Go unpastured, my lambs: your master now heeds not your bleating.
Now all lonely I wander over the fields and the pastures,
Or where the branchy shades are densest down in the valleys;
There I wait till late, while the shower and the storm-blast above me
Moan at their will, and sighings shake through the breaks of the woodlands.
 Go unpastured, my lambs: your master now heeds not your bleating.
Ah! how my fields, once neat, are now overgrown and unsightly,
Forward only in weeds, and the tall corn sickens with mildew!
Mateless, my vines droop down the shrivelled weight of their clusters;
Neither please me my myrtles; and even the sheep are a trouble;
They seem sad, and they turn their faces, poor things, to their master!
 Go unpastured, my lambs: your master now heeds not your bleating.
Tityrus calls to the hazels; to the ash-trees Alphesibœus;
Ægon suggests the willows: 'The streams,' says lovely Amyntas;
'Here are the cool springs, here the moss-broidered grass and the hillocks;
'Here are the zephyrs, and here the arbutus whispers the ripple.'

These things they sing to the deaf; so I took to the thickets and
    left them.
  Go unpastured, my lambs : your master now heeds not your
    bleating.
Mopsus addressed me next, for he had espied me returning
(Wise in the language of birds, and wise in the stars too, is
    Mopsus):
'Thyrsis,' he said, 'what is this? what bilious humour afflicts thee?
'Either love is the cause, or the blast of some star inauspicious;
'Saturn's star is of all the oftenest deadly to shepherds,
'Fixing deep in the breast his slant leaden shaft of sickness.'
  Go unpastured, my lambs : your master now heeds not your
    bleating.
Round me fair maids wonder ; 'What will come of thee, Thyrsis?
'What wouldst thou have?' they say : 'not commonly see we the
    young men
'Wearing that cloud on the brow, the eyes thus stern and the
    visage:
'Youth seeks the dance and sports, and in all will tend to be
    wooing :
'Rightfully so : twice wretched is he who is late in his loving.'
  Go unpastured, my lambs : your master now heeds not your
    bleating.
Dryope came, and Hyas, and Ægle, the daughter of Baucis
(Learned is she in the song and the lute, but O what a proud
    one !) ;
Came to me Chloris also, the maid from the banks of the Chelmer.
Nothing their blandishings move me, nothing their prattle of
    comfort ;
Nothing the present can move me, nor any hope of the future.
  Go unpastured, my lambs : your master now heeds not your
    bleating.
Ah me ! how like one another the herds frisk over the meadows,
All by the law of their kind, companions equally common ;
No one selecting for friendship this one rather than that one
Out of the flock ! So come in droves to their feeding the jackals ;
So in their turns pair also the rough untameable zebras.
Such too the law of the deep, where Proteus down on the shingle
Numbers his troops of sea-calves. Nay, that meanest of wing'd
    ones,
See how the sparrow has always near him a fellow, when flying

Round by the barns he chirrups, but seeks his own thatch ere it
    darkens;
Whom should fate strike lifeless—whether the beak of the falcon
Pin him in air, or he lie transfixed by the reed of the ditcher—
Quick the survivor is off, and a moment finds him remated.
We are the hard race, we, the battered children of fortune,
We of the breed of men, strange-minded and different-moulded!
Scarcely does any discover his one true mate among thousands;
Or, if kindlier chance shall have given the singular blessing,
Comes a dark day on the creep, and comes the hour unexpected,
Snatching away the gift, and leaving the anguish eternal.
    Go unpastured, my lambs: your master now heeds not your
        bleating.
Ah! what roaming whimsy drew my steps to a distance,
Over the rocks hung in air and the Alpine passes and glaciers!
Was it so needful for me to have seen old Rome in her ruins—
Even though Rome had been such as, erst in the days of her
    greatness,
Tityrus, only to visit, forsook both his flocks and his country—
That but for this I consented to lack the use of thy presence,
Placing so many seas and so many mountains between us,
So many woods and rocks and so many murmuring rivers?
Ah! at the end at least to have touched his hand had been given
    me,
Closed his beautiful eyes in the placid hour of his dying,
Said to my friend, 'Farewell! in the world of the stars think of *me*!'
    Go unpastured, my lambs: your master now heeds not your
        bleating.
Albeit also of *you* my memory never shall weary,
Swains of the Tuscan land, well-practised youths in the Muses,
Here there was grace and lightness; Tuscan *thou* too, my Damon,
Tracing the line of thy race from the ancient city of Lucca!
O, how mighty was I, when, stretched by the stream of the Arno
Murmuring cool, and where the poplar-grove softens the herbage,
Violets now I would pluck, and now the sprigs of the myrtle,
Hearing Menalcas and Lycidas vying the while in their ditties!
I also dared the challenge; nor, as I reckon, the hearers
Greatly disliked my trials—for yet the tokens are with me,
Rush-plaits, osier nets, and reed-stops of wax, which they gave me.
Ay more: two of the group have taught *our* name to their beech-
    woods—

Dati and also Francini, both of them notable shepherds,
As well in lore as in voice, and both of the blood of the Lydian.
   Go unpastured, my lambs: your master now heeds not your bleating.
Then too the pleasant dreams which the dewy moon woke within me,
Penning the young kids alone within their wattles at even!
Ah! how often I said, when already the black mould bewrapt thee,
'Now my Damon is singing, or spreading his snares for the leveret;
'Now he is weaving his twig-net for some of his various uses.'
What with my easy mind I hoped as then in the future
Lightly I seized with the wish and fancied as present before me.
'Ho, my friend!' I would cry: 'art busy? If nothing prevent thee,
'Shall we go rest somewhere in some talk-favouring covert,
'Or to the waters of Colne, or the fields of Cassibelaunus?
'There thou shalt run me over the list of thy herbs and their juices,
'Foxglove, and crocuses lowly, and hyacinth-leaf with its blossom,
'Marsh-plants also that grow for use in the art of the healer.'
Perish the plants each one, and perish all arts of the healer
Gotten of herbs, since nothing served they even their master!
I too—for strangely my pipe for some time past had been sounding
Strains of an unknown strength—'tis one day more than eleven since
Thus it befell—and perchance the reeds I was trying were new ones:
Bursting their fastenings, they flew apart when touched, and no farther
Dared to endure the grave sounds: I am haply in this overboastful;
Yet I will tell out the tale. Ye woods, yield your honours and listen!
   Go unpastured, my lambs: your master now heeds not your bleating.
I have a theme of the Trojans cruising our southern headlands
Shaping to song, and the realm of Imogen, daughter of Pandras,
Brennus and Arvirach, dukes, and Bren's bold brother, Belinus;
Then the Armorican settlers under the laws of the Britons,
Ay, and the womb of Igraine fatally pregnant with Arthur,

Uther's son, whom he got disguised in Gorlois' likeness,
All by Merlin's craft. O then, if life shall be spared me,
Thou shalt be hung, my pipe, far off on some brown dying pine-tree,
Much forgotten of me; or else yon Latian music
Changed for the British war-screech! What then? For one to do all things,
One to hope all things, fits not! Prize sufficiently ample
Mine, and distinction great (unheard of ever thereafter
Though I should be, and inglorious, all through the world of the stranger),
If but yellow-haired Ouse shall read me, the drinker of Alan,
Humber, which whirls as it flows, and Trent's whole valley of orchards,
Thames, my own Thames, above all, and Tamar's western waters,
Tawny with ores, and where the white waves swinge the far Orkneys.
  Go unpastured, my lambs: your master now heeds not your bleating.
These I was keeping for thee, wrapt up in the rind of the laurel,
These and other things with them; and mainly the two cups which Manso—
Manso, not the last of Southern Italy's glories —
Gave me, a wonder of art, which himself, a wonder of nature,
Carved with a double design of his own well-skilled invention:
Here the Red Sea in the midst, and the odoriferous summer,
Araby's winding shores, and palm trees sweating their balsams,
Mid which the bird divine, earth's marvel, the singular Phœnix,
Blazing cærulean-bright with wings of different colours,
Turns to behold Aurora surmounting the glassy-green billows:
Obverse is Heaven's vast vault and the great Olympian mansion.
Who would suppose it? Even here is Love and his cloud-painted quiver,
Arms glittering torch-lit, and arrows tipped with the fire-gem.
Nor is it meagre souls and the base-born breasts of the vulgar
Hence that he strikes; but, whirling round him his luminous splendours,
Always he scatters his darts right upwards sheer through the star-depths
Restless, and never deigns to level the pain of them downwards;
Whence the sacred minds and the forms of the gods ever-burning.

'Thou too art there—not vain is the hope that I cherish, my
    Damon—
Thou too art certainly there; for whither besides could have vanished
Holy-sweet fancies like thine, and purity stainless as thine was?
No; not down in Lethe's darkness ought we to seek thee!
Tears are not fitting for thee, nor for thee will we weep any longer;
Flow no more, ye tear-drops! Damon inhabits the ether;
Pure, he possesses the sky; he has spurned back the arc of the
    rainbow.
Housed mid the souls of the heroes, housed mid the gods ever-
    lasting,
Quaffs he the sacred chalices, drinks he the joys of the blessed,
Holy-mouthed himself. But O, Heaven's rights being now thine,
Be thou with me for my good, however I ought to invoke thee,
Whether still as our Damon, or whether of names thou wouldst
    rather
That of Diodati now, by which deep-meaning divine name
All the celestials shall know thee, while shepherds shall still call
    thee Damon.
For that the rosy blush and the unstained strength of young
    manhood
Ever were dear to thee, and the marriage joy never was tasted,
Lo! there are kept for thee the honours of those that were virgin!
Thou, with thy fair head crowned with the golden, glittering
    cincture,
Waving green branches of palm, and walking the gladsome pro-
    cession,
Aye shall act and repeat the endless heavenly nuptials,
There where song never fails, and the lyre and the dance mix to
    madness,
There where the revel rages and Sion's thyrsus beats time.'

www.ingramcontent.com/pod-product-compliance
Lightning Source LLC
Chambersburg PA
CBHW030337170426
43202CB00010B/1159